TALKING DRUMS

▼▼▼▼▼▼▼▼▼▼▼▼▼▼▼▼▼▼▼▼▼▼▼▼▼▼▼▼▼▼▼

Reading and Writing with African American Stories, Spirituals, and Multimedia Resources

Wanda Cobb Finnen

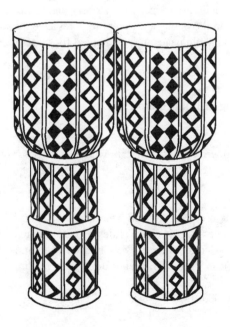

TEACHER IDEAS PRESS
Portsmouth, NH

With a debt of gratitude and love I can never hope to repay,
I dedicate Talking Drums *to my mother, Alverta Mae Cobb,*
for expecting excellence and stirring up the gifts of
language and music within my soul.

Teacher Ideas Press
A division of Reed Elsevier Inc.
361 Hanover Street
Portsmouth, NH 03801–3912
www.teacherideaspress.com

Offices and agents throughout the world

Library of Congress Cataloging-in-Publication Data

Finnen, Wanda Cobb.
    Talking drums : reading and writing with African American stories, spirituals, and multimedia
resources / Wanda Cobb Finnen.
        p. cm.
    ISBN 1-59158-057-9
    1. African Americans—Folklore. 2. African Americans—History. 3. African Americans—
Social life and customs. 4. Tales—Africa. 5. Tales—United States. 6. Oral tradition—United
States. 7. Spirituals (Songs)—United States. 8. Children's literature, African (English)
9. Children's literature, American. 10. Children—Books and reading. I. Title.
GR111.A47F564 2003
398'.089'96073—dc22   2003014894

Editor: Suzanne Barchers
Production Coordinator: Angela Laughlin
Typesetter: Westchester Book Services
Cover design: Gaile Ivaska
Manufacturing: Steve Bernier

Printed in the United States of America on acid-free paper

08 07 06 05 04 VP 1 2 3 4 5

Contents

Acknowledgments

Every stream has its source.

—Mayombe proverb

Drum Majors: Dr. Joyce Armstrong Carroll and Mr. Eddie Wilson;

Talking Drummers: PW, BT, BM, PP, DD, DA, SF, and DW;

Friends and Confidants: Jessie, Mary Lou, Tynia Marie, and Holly;

Teacher Ideas Press Acquisitions Editor, Suzanne Barchers;

Pastor/Teacher, Dr. Shaun Lebarron Moton;

My husband of more than thirty years, Larry E. Finnen;

Sons, Paul and Timothy; Granddaughters, Shayna and Triniti;

"Jesus the Author and Finisher of [my] faith" (Hebrews 12:2).

IN REMEMBRANCE

A sandstorm passes, the stars remain.

—African proverb

Daddy, James Walter Cobb,

for seeing the princess within the pumpkin;

Sister, Sheila Yvette, mentor and role model,

for inspiring me to sing Zion's songs in times of sorrow—

The sandstorm has passed; your stars remain. I remember.

Were You There?: Prologue

If the drum is not made, it is the fault of the master.
If it is not beaten, it is the fault of the drummers.
—Nigerian proverb

Were You There?

Were you there when they crucified my Lord?
Were you there when they crucified my Lord?
Oh-oh, oh-oh, sometimes it causes me to tremble, tremble.
Were you there when they crucified my Lord?

Were you there when they nailed Him to the tree?
Were you there when they nailed Him to the tree?
Oh-oh, oh-oh, sometimes it causes me to tremble, tremble.
Were you there when they nailed Him to the cross?

Were you there when they pierced Him in the side?
Were you there when they pierced Him in the side?
Oh-oh, oh-oh, sometimes it causes me to tremble, tremble.
Were you there when they pierced Him in the side?

Were you there when the sun refused to shine?
Were you there when the sun refused to shine?
Oh-oh, oh-oh, sometimes it causes me to tremble, tremble.
Were you there when the sun refused to shine?

Were you there when they laid Him in the tomb?
Were you there when they laid Him in the tomb?
Oh-oh, oh-oh, sometimes it causes me to tremble, tremble.
Were you there when they laid Him in the tomb?

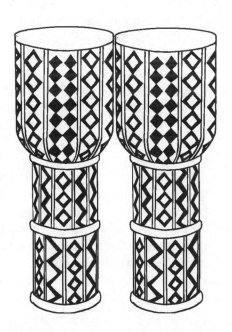

TALKING DRUMS

Drums have accentuated the pulse of human history since at least 6000 B.C. Primitive drums made of hollowed tree trunks, gourds, or clay, covered with the taut skins of goats, sheep, snakes, cows, or other animals, have played a central role in religious ceremonies, rituals, initiations, celebrations, and communication in Africa. Indeed, drums underscore the rhythmic music that punctuates African and African American history.

On the expansive African continent in days of old, the magic of talking drums allowed villages to signal and communicate with one another. The hourglass-shaped talking drums of West Africa emulated spoken language to convey messages. Since as early as the tenth century, talking drummers, or griots, have safeguarded the treasured chronicles of their tribes. Though the drums did not make the arduous journey across the Atlantic Ocean, the gift of storytelling passed on to succeeding generations of New World griots.

Stolen from their homeland, deprived of talking drums, and stymied from continuing the revered African oral tradition in a strange land, these displaced *djelis*, these folklore custodians, endeavored to keep their stories and music alive. Conceived in the bowels of slave ships, born on the auction block, nursed in the cotton fields, and weaned in the slave quarters of the American South, the heir to African folklore emerged. Africans in America nourished the infant African American oral tradition in their churches and homes. Spirituals, tales of the old land, family genealogies, legends, slave narratives, and freedmen's tales head this family tree. Regrettably, this unique African American oral tradition did not trigger a proliferation of mainstream literature featuring African Americans until the last decade of the twentieth century.

The twentieth- and twenty-first-century authors, poets, artists, and storytellers who beautifully recount the African American saga exemplify the spirit of the griots. Langston Hughes, Gwendolyn Brooks, Zora Hurston, Eloise Greenfield, Mildred Taylor, Ashley Bryan, Angela Johnson, Floyd Cooper, Angela Shelf Medearis, Maya Angelou, Toyomi Igus, Alice Walker, Isabell Monk, Virginia Hamilton, Andrea Pinkney, Patricia McKissack, Faith Ringgold, Walter Dean Myers, Toni Morrison, and countless others play a part in the intricate talking drum system narrating the African American role in American history. The circle of griots swells with the passage of time. The messages of this illustrious band beckon readers to listen to the stories of Africa's scattered children.

The stories of African Americans enhance the American story. Only when the voices of all Americans are heard will the American story be perfected. Proverbs, traditional spirituals, folklore, picture books, storybooks, nonfiction books, videos, Web sites, and varied writing response opportunities can take you there, to the language of the talking drums.

1
▼▼▼▼▼

Rock-a My Soul: Introduction

If we forget yesterday, how shall we remember tomorrow?
—Nigerian proverb

Rock-a My Soul

Rock-a my soul in the bosom of Abraham.
Rock-a my soul in the bosom of Abraham.
Rock-a my soul in the bosom of Abraham.
Oh, rock-a my soul!

When I went down to the valley to pray.
Oh, rock-a my soul.
My soul got happy and I stayed all day.
Oh, rock-a my soul!

Rock-a my soul in the bosom of Abraham.
Rock-a my soul in the bosom of Abraham.
Rock-a my soul in the bosom of Abraham.
Oh, rock-a my soul!

Rock-a my soul in the bosom of Abraham.
Rock-a my soul in the bosom of Abraham.
Rock-a my soul in the bosom of Abraham.
Oh, rock-a my soul!

OH, ROCK-A MY SOUL

Rock, rock-a my soul. Rock, rock-a my soul. Rock, rock-a my soul. Oh, rock-a my soul! Rousing, reverberating rhythms rock the souls of Motherland Africa's children as honored djeli, *the royal bards of humanity's firstborn, rehearse civilization's stories. Drum language in rich, percussive tones resonates from drums carved of gourds, cedar, mahogany, or ebony, covered with the hides of cows, goats, or reptiles. Proverbs, family genealogies, magical myths, histories, and ancient tales rock the soul of Æthiopia's beloved offspring, flung across the seven continents by history's happenings.*

LISTEN TO THE TALKING DRUMS: AN INVITATION

Prepare to hear a symphony of talking drums, tuned and ready to transport the reader from Uganda to Ghana to Nigeria to Kenya to Harlem to Birmingham, and to the South Carolina and Georgia Sea Islands. Dive to the bottom of the sea off the Florida coast and explore the wreckage of the slave ship *Henrietta Marie*. Toil in the heat of the day on southern plantations for no wages and even less dignity. Sing sorrow's songs in the midnight moments of tribulation. Travel terrified and bone-tired on the Underground Railroad in the shadows of nighttime. Sit inside the highest court in the land of the free and witness justice weighed. Rejoice on sun-soaked fields and streets as Jubilee makes a long anticipated arrival on Texas turf. Listen as sorrow's songs modulate to joy's descant.

Hunger for justice in the world's greatest democracy. Walk by a drinking fountain labeled "White only" and thirst for water. Wait in anguish outside a church in Birmingham as firemen carry out the lifeless bodies of four young girls who will not live to see another Sunday. Stand among the expectant masses in the nation's capitol and hear a dream unveiled. Watch merging cultures and crumbling barriers in fulfillment of the drum major's dream. Allow the drums' stories to rock your soul.

FOLKLORE

The First Djeli and His Talking Drum
(Inspired by the Native American Seneca tale,
"The Storytelling Stone," and African oral tradition)

▼▼▼▼▼

Long before long ago, before Great Grandmother Africa cradles my ancestors on her ample, nurturing bosom, before drums have a voice, oppressive silence holds hostage a village on the Ivory Coast of West Africa. Grief and taut discouragement silence the villagers' laughter. No care-free, healthy children run and play in the village. As the coolness of daybreak surrenders to the menacing midday sun, men and women whose dancing feet have lost their rhythm slump against their mud-thatched huts weary and disheartened. Even Buka, spirit of the sky, sulks like a spoiled child, splitting the heavens with clashes of thunder and flashes of lightning in his momentary temper tantrums but releasing no life-giving rain.

Too long the dry season lingers, taunting the villagers in their helplessness like a lion toying with its prey before devouring it. The most ancient of the elders sit discouraged and weak, too tired to live, too stubborn to die. A handful of those of too many years or too few days, those feeble ones have died in the past weeks. Death, ever democratic, shows no favoritism in choosing its target. Between midnight and dawn for a week of days the thief stealthily and mercilessly enters one hut after another, finally crossing Chief Kwame's threshold to claim his beloved infant daughter, Amma.

In the nearby forest the healthy young men not yet overcome by the intense, devilish heat cut down sturdy, mahogany trees, and the young girls and boys gather the wood to fuel the cooking fires. The chief's first-born son, ribbons of sweat falling from the top of his head, labors with the men hard at work. While swinging his ax with strength equal to what his father possessed as a young man, At-mun hears a low voice. At-mun ceases his work, looks all around him, behind the tree, and up in the tree. Seeing no one, At-mun continues to chop down the tree. Once more, At-mun hears the dis-embodied voice; again he searches for the speaker. The sound resonates from the bowels of the aged tree and causes a rumble in At-mun's belly, but At-mun sees no man to match the voice.

"Who speaks? Show yourself. Have you no respect? We've no time to play tricks," At-mun demands. Frustrated and endowed with the impatience of youth, At-mun angrily resumes his chore hacking at the old mahogany.

"I can help you more than you know. Before you hack into me again with your ax, listen to me," the phantom voice urges.

With the speed of the cheetah, young At-mun drops his ax and questions the tree. "How can you, a mere tree help me? I am the first-born son of Chief Kwame. What can you do that my father cannot do? He governs this tribe wisely. What do you have that he does not already possess? This forest belongs to my father. My father, Chief Kwame, holds power and authority in his hands."

"Yes, but you and your father have no power to restore joy to grieving mothers and hope to the disheartened. Your father gives leadership to the Hausa people. The men and women of your village work together to provide rice, plantains, and meat for your people. You use the wood of this forest to cook your food and the bark to clothe yourselves, but you cannot give happiness."

"Tell me what you can do," At-mun begs. "My mother wails with grief and refuses to eat. Can you place my darling sister Amma back into the arms of my mother? Can you breathe new life into the nostrils of the others stolen away by death? Do you possess healing oils to bathe feverish brows? The wisdom of the ages is shut up in the mouths of the grandmothers and grandfathers who have no strength to prophesy. Will the skies open at your command and pour out rain and renew their strength?"

"At-mun, the seasons of life must come and go. Life slips into death for all living creatures at a time appointed by one greater than I. Yet, I offer your people a way to hold fast to the spirits of your ancestors and to live forever in the hearts of your grandchildren's grandchildren.

Take your firewood and your bark from me for clothing, but set aside a portion of my trunk. Hollow out this trunk. Cover the ends with goat's hide, and make a drum. When a child comes into the world, play the drum. When the young child loses his first tooth, play the drum. When the young boy becomes a man, play the drum. As your young girls enter womanhood, sound the drums. When you worship the High God, play the drum. When you dance, play the drum. When you tell the story of your people, play the drum. My spirit will live on in the drum, and your spirit will live on in the telling."

Hastening to his father's home, At-mun shares the message of the talking tree. "Father, Father, I have heard the voice of the spirit of the mighty tree that stands in the center of the forest!"

With Chief Kwame's permission, At-mun follows the talking tree's instructions and fashions West Africa's first talking drum. That night Chief Kwame calls the village together. At-mun tells the villagers of his experience in the forest. With his talking drum, Africa's first djeli (storyteller) soothes the village that night and appeases the tree's spirit. Tales of the grandfathers and grand-mothers echo through the village.

Since that night, drums speak as the djeli relate the history of the sons and daughters of West Africa. Thus begins the epic saga of the African djeli and the talking drums.

▾▾▾▾▾   ı

ANCIENT AFRICAN ORAL TRADITION

Oral tradition is as ancient as the world in which we live. Since God first spoke the world into existence and pronounced satisfaction with His creation, the word has possessed power to create, sustain life, curse, bless, and revive. Traditional African societies born on humanity's birthplace have historically revered and sought to preserve the oral arts. As the United States of America annually pays homage with the Oscar to big screen storytellers and the stories they tell, Africa's ancient civilizations hold their orators in the highest regard.

All of the earth's children on each of the seven continents want stories. So it has always been. So it will continue. The Zulu have their legends about First Man and First Woman's quest for stories. West Africa has multiple stories of the trickster tortoise and of Ananse the Spider seeking to hoard all wisdom and corner the market on stories. Stories are more than idle diversions; stories elevate humanity above the beasts of the field and the birds of the air.

The legendary pharaohs, the Queen of Sheba, Cleopatra, Shaka Zulu, the legendary Baganda King Kintu, Sundiata, and King Prester John, tales of Anansi the Spider, proverbs for every known religion and civilization of the African continent, myths, Kanga writings with a more bountiful collection of fascinating folktales and fairy tales than all of Aesop's fables and Grimms' fairy tales, Africa has an ancient, enduring treasure trove of folklore.

Africa's oral tradition proved indestructible in the face of the onslaught of foreign invasion, the defacing of her land, and the plunder of her people. African folktales reflect the innumerable, religious influences on the African continent: Judeo–Christian, Islamic, Yoruba, and a host of others. Common main characters are the high god, the sky god, and Ananse or Anansi, the spider god. As with Greek, Native American, and European oral tradition, African myths, folktales, and folk literature commonly use animals to portray human characteristics. Smaller, less significant animals outsmart the more powerful animals. Ananse or Anansi, the spider, and the tortoise most often play the part of the clever tricksters.

The coffers of African folklore overflow with wise sayings, riddles, rhymes, superstitions, religious beliefs, songs, dances, customs, recipes, folktales, legends, and creation myths. African folklore accomplishes the purpose of both time capsule and portal. The proverbs, myths, folktales, superstitions, and customs uncover the soul of Africa, the values and philosophies of the people, as with the Nigerian proverb introducing this chapter. Some folktales and legends carry the reader back to indigenous Africa before the influx of Arabian and European visitors. Myths reflect primitive religious beliefs that have influenced and, in many cases, merged with Islamic and Christian practices. The values most treasured by indigenous African cultures resurface in the stories and sayings earlier generations bestowed on their descendants, an invaluable, incorruptible inheritance.

AFRICAN AMERICAN ORAL TRADITION

Although foreign invaders stole from Africa her precious gold, ivory, diamonds, exotic animals, and her healthy sons and daughters, the legacy of oral tradition was not lost. Those who stayed behind on the Ivory Coast of West Africa and those who crossed over have preserved and passed their stories on to others in a grapevine that has survived both the Middle Passage and the passage of time. The proud, distinctive art of African oral tradition has carried over into African American folklore. Anansi becomes "Aunt Nancy" in the New World versions of the prankish spider folk stories. Uncle Remus tales, the Gullah legends, slave songs, and folktales of bigger-than-life characters like freedom fighters and slaves outwitting their masters give African American folk literature its own flavor. African cultural influence also reveals itself in the rousing African American style of preaching exemplified by the sermons of James Weldon Johnson and the rhythmic, high-spirited, call-and-response worship services of many African American churches.

HOW TO USE THIS BOOK

The suggested literature and lesson ideas of *Talking Drums* lend themselves beautifully to teacher preparation courses, college-level multicultural literature or African American literature courses, grades 3 through 12 English/language arts classes, reading classes, reading and writing workshops, the social studies classroom, and to humanities classrooms. *Talking Drums* can serve as the course curriculum for a 45- to 50-minute-per-day yearlong class or for a 90-minute-block semester course. To correlate with the study of U.S. history, the English/language arts or high school humanities teacher may choose to present the chapters as sequenced, selecting from the fiction and nonfiction texts and from the recommended multimedia in each chapter. As the drum major in your classroom, modify the following unit lesson plans to fit the needs of your students.

Chapter Layout

Each chapter, centered on either a stage of African American history or a facet of African American life, begins with a proverb followed by a traditional spiritual that holds both heavenly and earthly meanings. These spirituals have played an essential role in the African American saga and set the tone for each chapter or literary selection. Background information then provides the historical context for the literature, followed by a Mind Mixer (discussion, prewriting, graphic organizer) that serves as an informal diagnosis of students' attitudes toward and prior knowledge of that chapter's topic. Next, the vocabulary list draws the students' attention to the new words they may encounter as they read the literature and explore the multimedia discussed later in the chapter. African and African American folklore retellings herald the literary selections. In each chapter students will also learn about traditional African or African American food and conduct research and complete writing assignments related to the food.

With recognized state, national, and international standards in mind (see Appendixes A and B), *Talking Drums* presents culturally diverse narrative, expository, and nonprint text suggestions in addition to multimedia resources. In the strictest sense, all the literature suggestions in this book do not qualify as African American because some of the authors are not African American, but the stories told and the truths revealed reflect the African American experience.

Wondrously illustrated picture books head the suggested texts. Storytelling has the power to entertain, provoke thought, evoke emotions, and inform. Because of their brevity, picture books fit into the busiest teacher's schedule, with time after reading to discuss and respond to the text. I have read picture books to both gifted and challenged middle schoolers, to high school students, to college students in teacher prep classes, and to teachers across Texas. Picture books present a theme, introduce an area of study, inform, and enrich, and they can be read and responded to within a 45- to 60-minute class. Additional texts referenced in each chapter include novels, nonfiction, and multimedia. The literature ranges from classics like Booker T. Washington's *Up from Slavery* (1901) and James Weldon Johnson's *God's Trombones* (1927) to Mildred D. Taylor's *The Land* (2001).

Most of the picture book summaries in *Talking Drums* conclude with a suggested *objet trouve* (treasured object) to distribute to each student. The *objet trouve* brings closure to the lesson and also acts as a concrete muse to stimulate the student's minds to write. Teachers can order these items from catalog like U.S. Toys, buy them in a craft store, find them in a dollar store, or make an Ellison die-cut of the treasure. In a craft store you can find these treasures in sponge and felt cut-outs, miniature collectibles, ready-made die-cuts, buttons and other accessories intended for clothing, party favors, pencils, and stickers. Joyce Armstrong Carroll and Edward Wilson, co-directors of the New Jersey Writing Project in Texas, advocate culminating a reading experience with tangible, visible representations of the literature to help learners of all ages make meaningful connections.

Reader Response Opportunities are provided for both print and multimedia suggestions. Reader response opportunity suggestions range from prewriting strategies and graphic organizers to open-ended questions, visual representations, research assignments, and projects. Modify the response suggestions to match your students' needs and abilities. The picture book reader response opportunities may be adjusted to implement at any grade level, from primary to adult writing workshops. Primary level children can draw a picture in response to the story or discuss the story orally.

Each chapter concludes with elementary, secondary, and multilevel writing prompts. Students should take the writing prompts through the entire writing process: prewriting, drafting, conferencing, revising, editing, and publishing. In the appendixes at the back of this book, you will find model rubrics to assess the writing activities.

This book is designed for the teacher to either work through each chapter or to select books and related ideas randomly. Any single literary selection and its accompanying writing opportunities in this book can additionally stand alone as one day's lesson. I hope you, the teacher and reader, will use *Talking Drums* freely throughout the academic year, integrating the literature found here into a multicultural curriculum, and not only once a year during February's Black History Month. May your classroom celebrate and validate the stories of all children, inspiring each to listen to the talking drums. The students will not forget what they see and feel as the talking drums speak to their hearts.

STRATEGIES FOR TEACHING THE UNITS

Proverb

1. Write the proverb on the board or on a sentence strip.
2. Have students copy the proverb into their reflections log with their thoughts about the proverb.
3. Discuss the proverb.

Traditional Spiritual

1. Give students a copy of the traditional spiritual or read it aloud.
2. When possible, let the students hear the spiritual sung.
3. Assign the reader response opportunity when indicated.

Mind Mixer

Use the Mind Mixer to help both you and your students gauge their knowledge and attitude about the topic.

Vocabulary

1. After the thematic proverb and traditional spiritual in each chapter is a list of terms introduced in the chapter or necessary for responding to the print and nonprint texts.

2. Make the word list available to the students at the beginning of the unit of study.

3. Make students aware of the word list, but avoid having students look up and define unknown words out of context. Instead, challenge them to discover the meanings of these words as used in context through interaction with the text. Most words and terms are defined or explained in the context of the expository text of each chapter.

Folklore

1. Read the story.

2. Divide the students into small groups or pairs and have them complete the Folklore Charts or assign them the appropriate Reader Response Opportunity.

Traditional Food Fare

1. Read the introductory information about the food.

2. Assign the Reader Response Opportunity.

3. When possible prepare and/or sample the food with your students.

Book Selections

For every selected text suggestion in this book there is a book review that includes the title, the name of the author, publishing information, and honors or awards received. Major literary awards are listed below.

Major Honors/Awards

Pulitzer Prize: literature or journalism

Nobel Prize: literature

American Library Association (ALA)

Newbery: children's and young adult literature

Caldecott: illustrations in children's/young adult literature

Coretta Scott King: children's author/illustrator of African descent

Notable ALA Trade Book

International Reading Association (IRA)

Notable Children's Books: NCTE (National Council of Teachers of English)

Golden Kite Award: Society of Children's Book Writers and Illustrators

National Book Award

Carter G. Woodson Award

Scott O'Dell Award for Historical Fiction

Read the picture book, novel excerpt, or suggested portions of nonfiction texts aloud. Reading experts Lucy Calkins, author of *The Art of Teaching Reading* (2001), and Jim Trelease, author of *The Read-Aloud Handbook* (1995), emphasize the multiple benefits of reading aloud to students of all ages in the classroom on a regular basis. Everyone benefits from a story.

Picture Book

1. Show students the cover and read aloud the title, author, illustrator's names, and the dedication. Students need to know all of these elements of a book.
2. Let students make predictions about what might happen in the book.
3. Read aloud the book to your class.
4. Distribute the *objet trouve*.
5. Discuss the connection of the *objet trouve* to the book.
6. Assign the appropriate Reader Response Opportunity.

Novels/Nonfiction

1. Read an excerpt from the novel, full-length narrative, or expository nonfiction selection.
2. Take your students to the library to check out a book on the same topic, pass out copies of the selected book, or read a portion of the book aloud daily to the students.
3. Assign the appropriate Reader Response Opportunity.

Multimedia: Internet/Video

Multimedia suggestions include Web sites, videos, and music.

1. Introduce the Web site or video and explain its relationship to the unit of study or suggested texts in the chapter.
2. Have students view the video or site.
3. Assign the Reader Response Opportunity.
4. Let students work independently in the classroom, library, computer lab, or at home.

Note: If you cannot access a suggested Web site, simply type in the keyword/subject to find sites on the same topic.

Reader Response Opportunities

Prewriting Strategies

Prewriting strategies function equally well both as an icebreaker before exploring the text or after reading and interacting in response to the text. The flow of ideas takes precedence over concern with mechanical errors or conventions of language. Teachers can explain and model a particular strategy with the whole class, allow students to work in pairs or small groups of 3 to 5, and give a set amount of time for students to complete the task alone or with others. Use a kitchen timer or an overhead transparency timer to keep track of time.

- **Brainstorming:** Solicit answers on a given topic or idea from the class to jumpstart thinking. Either you or a volunteer student should record the answers on the board, chart tablet, or transparency as students call out responses. Record all responses given without comment or judgment from the teacher or classmates.
- **Folklore Chart:** The Folklore Chart allows the student to interpret, analyze, and evaluate folk literature. You will find a model in Appendix E.

- **Listing:** Each individual learner lists what comes to mind on a given topic. For example, "List every animal you might see in West Africa."

- **Text Reflection Log:** Students keep a log in a spiral notebook and record their reflections on and reactions to text or media. Students can ask questions, comment on a character's actions, predict plot, discuss how the text relates to their lives, and compare and contrast the text or events and characters from the text to other literature and media. The log may also be used for prewriting and graphic organizers (see below).

- **Thought Completion** (Carroll & Wilson, 1993): Students complete an open-ended sentence fragment. Examples:

    "I feel free when I —————————."

    "When I think about Paul-Edward in *The Land* (Taylor, 2001),

    I feel like —————————."

Graphic Organizers

A graphic organizer, patterned prewriting, allows the learner not only to record his or her thoughts and details but also to manipulate these ideas to reflect their relationship to each other. Teachers should explain the graphic organizer and model using it. Perhaps show the samples below. Students can then construct the graphic organizer themselves rather than filling in a ready-made copy. This helps the reader and writer process and analyze the information (Hyerle, 1996).

- **Bio Graph:** The Bio Graph registers high and low points in a writer or a character's life, much like a bar graph or an EKG reading in an ICU room. The writer adds an explanation of the highs and lows. See, below, Bio Graph on Phyllis Wheatley, who was born in Senegal and achieved fame as a poet in the United States.

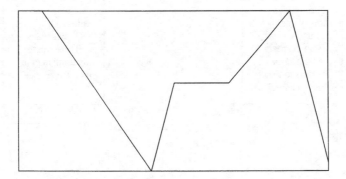

Phillis Wheatley Bio Graph. The birth of any child was a high point in Phillis Wheatley's Senegal. The extended family and clan traditionally gathers for child-naming ceremonies. The abrupt plunge in the graph represents the abduction and enslavement of Phillis at the age of eight years old. The rise after the first low reflects the joy and wonder young Phillis probably experiences as she studies with the Wheatley children in their home and continues as she begins to write poetry. Her trip to London and the publication of her book of verse produce another rise. The final low point comes at Ms. Wheatley's death in 1784. © 2004 Wanda Finnen

- **Cluster:** The cluster allows the reader to arrange traits/details, as seen in the figure below. Place the focal point of the topic in either the center circle or in the top circle. Add as many circles as needed.

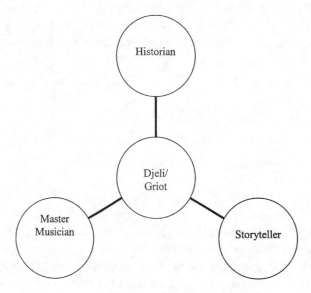

- **Cycle Graph:** The Cycle Graph shows the pattern or cycle of repetition in folk literature. Note the example in the figure below based on the Ashanti legend, "Talk, Talk."

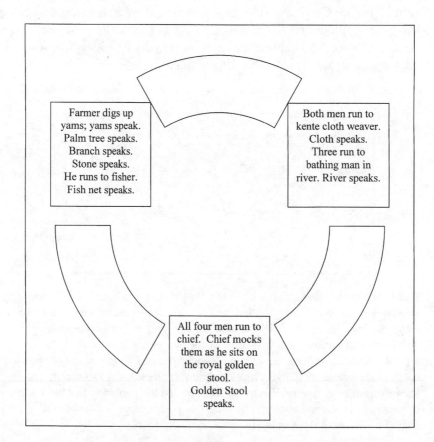

Cycle Graph "Talk, Talk." © 2004 Wanda Finnen

- **KWL Chart:** The **KWL** chart serves as both an informal pretest/diagnostic tool and an informal posttest. At the onset of a unit of study, students list what they know about a topic in the **K** column and what they want to know in the **W** column. In the **L** column students list new learning. See the model below on Swahili.

K	W	L
African language	How to speak it	East African
Spoken by many	How to understand	Called Kiswahili
Jambo: hello	Numbers in Swahili	*Rafiki:* friend
Simba: lion	Words for *book, God*	*Baba:* father

- **Ring Graph:** The reader/writer charts a precipitating event and the progression of events that evolve from the initial occurrence; it is excellent for registering cause and effect or conflict and resolution. Add as many outer rings as necessary. See the example below on the Fisk Jubilee Singers.

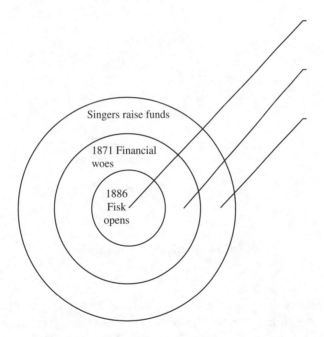

Jubilee Singers. © 2004 Wanda Finnen

- **T-Chart:** A T-chart allows the reader/writer to analyze two sides of an issue, the pros and cons, and to organize similarities and differences. The example below contrasts Booker T. Washington with W. E. B. Du Bois.

Booker T. Washington	W. E. B. Du Bois
Educator	Historian/activist
Founder of Tuskegee	Helped form Niagra Movement
For vocational education	For intellectual "Talented Tenth"
Up from Slavery	*The Souls of Black Folk*

- **Timeline:** A timeline chronologically lists the pivotal events of a person's life or of significant events/periods in history. For example, below is a model timeline of the life of trailblazer African American poet Phillis Wheatley.

  c. 1753   Born in Senegal
  c. Age 8 Brought to U.S. as a slave Educated in Wheatley household
  1770   First poem published
  1773   Book published, England
  1784   Published "Liberty and Peace"
  1784   Died

- **Venn Diagram:** A Venn diagram consists of two or more overlapping geometric figures and makes an excellent tool for recording similarities and differences.

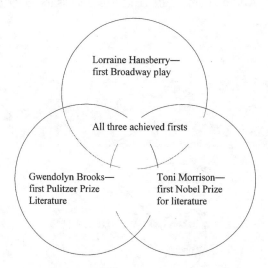

African American Women Djelis

- **Web:** A web allows the writer to organize traits of a character or place. The reader/writer writes the topic of description inside the oval, for example, *West African Nations.* Then, in each space the reader/writer lists characteristics of the topic. Additional lines should extend from the subtopics as the writer generates specific details.

Open-Ended Response Opportunity

The Open-Ended Response Opportunity promotes problem solving and critical thinking, gives writing practice, and teaches students to reflect on literature and express themselves. Focus on content and grade-level appropriate grammar and language usage. A rubric is provided at the back of this book to assess open-ended responses.

- Assign the Open-Ended Response.
- Allow students to ask questions for clarification.
- Advise students of the expectations by sharing the rubric.

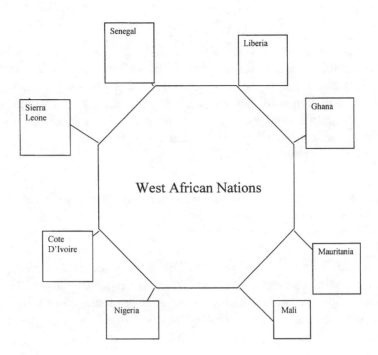

- Allow appropriate time for students to answer the question(s).
- Assess the question(s) using the rubric. Content ranks supreme in these answers. Answers may vary, but insist that students explain and support them. *Metacognition,* a learner thinking about and understanding how she or he arrives at a response, develops a student's critical thinking skills.

Writing Prompt

Talking Drums presents two or more writing prompts per chapter. If a lengthy writing assignment follows the reading of every piece of literature, students will lose the simple joy of the stories. However, students do need to take at least one composition through the writing process each grading period. The components of the writing process appear in bold letters. Remember, writing is not a linear process with sequential stages but rather a recursive cycle. For example, after prewriting the student may decide on a different approach to the prompt. During a conference, ideas may come to the writer, which may then lead to another draft.

Writing Prompt Prewriting

- Read the writing prompt to your students or have them read it silently.
- Prewrite to the prompt using one of the strategies suggested in this text.
- Discuss possible approaches to the prompt (descriptive, narrative, explanatory, classificatory, persuasive).
- Emphasize the directions and go over the rubric with the students.
- Encourage your students to refer to the previously completed prewriting strategies or graphic organizers and the completed open-ended responses.
- Allow time for prewriting.

Draft

Assign the writing prompt and allow sufficient class time for students to write. Have students focus on articulating, supporting, and organizing their ideas. Time for proofreading and editing language conventions, mechanics, and grammar will come later. However, you may have writers who see a red, hexagonal stop sign until they know the correct spelling of a word. Give the learner's needs first place; if frustration at not knowing a correct spelling blocks a student's writing process, let him or her look up the word in a dictionary or consult a classmate.

Conferences

Make the conferences student-led, with a student asking specific questions or addressing specific issues in his or her writing.

- *Peer conferences:* Before placing students in their conference groups, remind them to respect their classmates and their writings. Divide the students into small groups of three or four and have them each read aloud their own writing. For younger children, pairs work best. Assign a specific of the writing for the group to focus on or have the writer ask the group specific questions about the writing.
- *Micro-conference:* During writing time the teacher/facilitator should be available for Micro-conferences, circulating around the room and conducting brief conferences on the spot.

Revisions

After conferences conclude, student writers revise their compositions. Conferences can reoccur as needed.

Proofreading/Editing

Let students do peer editing. Spelling and grammar tools on computers have their usefulness, but they fall short in recognizing word choice errors such as the misuse of homonyms and confusion between possessive pronouns and pronoun contractions.

Submission/Assessment

Students submit their completed compositions. Use the holistic rubric in the appendixes to grade the compositions.

Go Tell It:
African American Storytellers

Until lions have their own storytellers, tales of the hunt will always glorify the hunter.

—Ibo proverb

Go Tell It on the Mountain

Go tell it on the mountain over the hills and everywhere.
Go tell it on the mountain that Jesus Christ is born.

While shepherds kept their watching o'er silent flocks by night,
Rang out the angel chorus that hailed our Savior's birth.

Go tell it on the mountain over the hills and everywhere.
Go tell it on the mountain that Jesus Christ is born.

Down in a lowly manger, the humble Christ was born,
And God sent us salvation that blessed Christmas morn.

Go tell it on the mountain over the hills and everywhere.
Go tell it on the mountain that Jesus Christ is born.

HISTORICAL CONTEXT

Heirs to the proud tradition of thousands of years of West African mansas, djelis, and griots continue to entertain and enlighten audiences both intimate and immeasurable. Self-appointed family historians record births, deaths, and the varied occasions in between, taking places of honor at family reunions, funerals, and informal gatherings. Grandmothers, great aunts, and grandpas share clouded memories of "I remember when . . ." A precious, inspired, anointed few have received the calling to tell their stories on the mountains, over the hills, and everywhere.

They answer to *nyamakalaw* or *nyama*-handler, *nyamakale, mansa, sanbanyi, yembe, djembefola, okyeame, bambara, balafola, griot, jeli,* or *djeli,* talking drummers—exotic names attached to Africa's time-honored story handlers and official spokespersons. These walking, breathing depositories of oral tradition serve as timeless connections between eternities past and eternities present, links between Old World Africa and New World America. The following list of notable African American authors can help you expand your classroom library. The list is not all inclusive, as fresh names emerge continually.

African American Authors

Maya Angelou Poet at President Bill Clinton's first presidential inauguration

> *A Song Flung up to Heaven* (2002)
>
> *Kofi and His Magic* (1996)
>
> *All God's Children Need Traveling Shoes* (1986)
>
> *Heart of a Woman* (1981)
>
> *I Know Why the Caged Bird Sings* (1969)

Cornelia Walker Bailey Sea island storyteller

> *God, Dr. Buzzard, and the Bolito Man* (2000)

James Baldwin Novelist on racial and social consciousness

> *Tell Me How Long the Train's Been Gone* (1968)
>
> *The Fire Next Time* (1963)
>
> *Nobody Knows My Name* (1961)
>
> *Notes of a Native Son* (1955)
>
> *Go Tell It on the Mountain* (1953)

Melba Pattillo Beals Congressional Gold Medallist

> *Warriors Don't Cry* (1994; Little Rock Nine memoirs)

Arna Bontemps Harlem Renaissance author

> *Story of the Negro* (1949 Newbery Honor Book)
>
> *God Sends Sunday* (1931)

Marie Bradby

> *More Than Anything Else* (1995)

Muriel Miller Branch

> *Juneteenth: Freedom Day* (1998)

Ruby Bridges School desegregation autobiographer

> *Through My Eyes* (1999; Jane Addams Children's Book Award 2000)

Gwendolyn Brooks Poet; first African American to receive a Pulitzer Prize

Annie Allen (1949)

Ashley Bryan Prolific and highly honored illustrator and storyteller

Ashley Bryan's ABC's of African American Poetry (1998 Coretta Scott King Illustrator Honor Book)

Climbing Jacob's Ladder (1991)

What a Morning!: The Christmas Story in Black Spirituals (1988 Coretta Scott King Illustrator Honor Book)

I'm Going to Sing: Black American Spirituals (1983 Coretta Scott King Illustrator Honor Book)

Beat the Story-Drum, Pum-Pum (1981 Coretta Scott King Illustrator Award Book)

The Dancing Granny (1977)

Walk Together, Children (1981, Coretta Scott King Award, Coretta Scott King Honor Book, ALA Notable Book)

Helen E. Buckley

Grandmother and I (1994)

Grandfather and I (1994)

Veronica Chambers

Amistad Rising: A Story of Freedom (1998)

Mama's Girl (1997; Book-of-the-Month Club, Best Book for Young Adults)

Evelyn Coleman

To Be a Drum (1998)

White Socks Only (1996; *Smithsonian Magazine* Notable Book for Children)

Floyd Cooper Author and illustrator; multiple recipient of Coretta Scott King Illustrator awards and honors

Coming Home: From the Life of Langston Hughes (1994; ALA Notable Book)

Michael H. Cottman Pulitzer Prize-winning journalist, 1992

Spirit Dive: An African American's Journey to Uncover a Sunken Slave Ship's Past (1999; formerly *The Wreck of the Henrietta Marie*)

Christopher Paul Curtis

Bud, Not Buddy (2000; Coretta Scott King Award; Newbery Honor Book)

The Watsons Go to Birmingham–1963 (1995; Newbery Honor Book, Coretta Scott King Honor Book, ALA Best Book)

Ossie Davis

Just Like Martin (1992)

Escape to Freedom (1979; Coretta Scott King Author Award)

Purlie Victorious (1961)

Leo and Diane Dillon Prolific, respected illustrators; 2003 Coretta Scott King Illustrator Honor recipients

Frederick Douglass Abolitionist, newspaper editor

Narrative of the Life of Frederick Douglass (1845)

Rita Dove Pulitzer Prize for poetry, 1987; youngest Poet Laureate in U.S. History; first African American Poet Laureate 1993–1995

W. E. B. Du Bois

The Souls of Black Folk (1903, 1994)

Paul Laurance Dunbar Dialectical poet

Complete Poems (1913; published posthumously)

Lyrics of Lowly Life (1896)

Oak and Ivy (1893)

Ralph Ellison

Invisible Man (1952; National Book Award for fiction, Presidential Medal of Freedom)

Oloudah Equiano

The Interesting Narrative of the Life of Oloudah Equiano, or Gustavus Vassa (1789)

Christine King Farris

My Brother Martin (2002)

Muriel Feelings

Moja Means One: A Swahili Counting Book (1972; Caldecott Honor Book)

Jambo Means Hello: A Swahili Alphabet Book (1975; Caldecott Honor Book)

Tom Feelings Caldecott Honor recipient 1972 and 1975; storyteller/illustrator on East African culture and Atlantic slave trade

The Middle Passage: White Ships Black Cargo (1999; Coretta Scott King Illustrator Award)

Valerie Flournoy

Patch Quilt (Coretta Scott King Illustrator Award, ALA Notable Book, 1986)

Tanya's Reunion (1996; IRA Teacher's Choice)

Ernest J. Gaines

A Lesson Before Dying (1997)

The Autobiography of Miss Jane Pittman (1971)

Henry Louis Gates, Jr. Chair, Afro-American Studies, Harvard University

Colored People (1994)

Nikki Giovanni Twentieth-century poet

Eloise Greenfield Poet

Grandpa's Face (1988; ALA Notable Book, School Library Best Book of the Year)

Africa Dream (1978; Coretta Scott King Author and Illustrator Award)

She Come Bringing Me That Little Baby Girl (1974)

Sister (1974; *New York Times* Outstanding Book of the Year)

Nikki Grimes

Talkin' About Bessie: The Story of Aviator Elizabeth Coleman (2003; Coretta Scott King Honor Book)

Bronx Masquerade (2003; Coretta Scott King Author Award)

Come Sunday (1996)

Alex Haley Special Pulitzer Prize 1977, NAACP Springarn Medal

> *Roots: The Saga of an American Family* (1976; National Book Award)
>
> *The Autobiography of Malcolm X* (1965)

Virginia Hamilton Descendant of slaves who fled north to Ohio

> *In the Beginning: Creation Stories from Around the World* (1988; Newbery Honor Book)
>
> *The People Could Fly* (1986; Coretta Scott King Author Award and Ilustrator Honor Book)
>
> *M.C. Higgins, the Great* (1975; Newbery Medal, National Book Award)
>
> *The House of Dies Drear* (1968)
>
> *Zeely* (1967)
>
> *Many Thousand Gone* (1995, 2002)

Lorraine Hansberry Playwright of first African American drama to win award as best play of the year

> *To Be Young Gifted and Black* (1969; autobiography)
>
> *A Raisin in the Sun* (1951; New York Drama Critics Award 1958–1959; 1974 Tony Award Best Musical)

Joyce Hansen

> *Which Way Freedom?* (1986; 1987 Coretta Scott King Honor Book, ALA Notable Book)

Jupiter Hammon First published African American poet, 1761

Jim Haskins Nonfiction author, Coretta Scott King Award recipient

> *Building a New Land: African Americans in Colonial America* (2001)
>
> *African Beginnings* (1998)
>
> *Black Eagles* (1995)
>
> *Outward Dreams: Black Inventors and Their Inventions* (1991)
>
> *The Cotton Club* (1977)
>
> *Black Music in America* (1987; Carter G. Woodson Award)

Sandy Lynne Holman School counselor, prevention coordinator

> *Is Everything Black Bad?* (1999)

Deborah Hopkinson

> *Sweet Clara and the Freedom Quilt* (1993; IRA Award)
>
> *A Band of Angels* (1999; *Smithsonian Magazine* Notable Book for Children; ALA Notable Book; NCTE Notable Book for a Global Society; Golden Kite Award book)

Elizabeth Fitzgerald Howard

> *Aunt Flossie's Hats* (1995)

Langston Hughes Harlem Renaissance poet and author

> *I Wonder as I Wander* (1956; autobiography)
>
> *The Dream Keeper* (1932)

Zora Hurston Curator of African American oral tradition

> *Dust Tracks on a Road* (1942)

Their Eyes Were Watching God (1937)

Mules and Men (1935)

Toyomi Igus

I See the Rhythm (1998; 1999 Coretta Scott King Illustrator Award)

Two Mrs. Gibsons (1996)

Angela Johnson

Daddy Calls Me Man (2000)

Toning the Sweep (1993; 1994 Coretta Scott King Award; 1993 *School Library Journal* Best Book)

The Leaving Morning (1992)

Tell Me a Story, Mama (1992; *School Library Journal* Best Book of the Year)

When I Am Old with You (1990; 1991 Coretta Scott King Author Honor Book)

Dinah Johnson

Quinnie Blue (2000)

Dolores Johnson

Now Let Me Fly (1997)

James Weldon Johnson First Executive Secretary of NAACP

The Creation (1995; Coretta Scott King Illustrator Book)

"Lift Every Voice and Sing," African American National Anthem (1921)

God's Trombones (1927)

Dr. Martin Luther King, Jr. Nobel Peace Prize winner

Martin's Big Words (2002; Coretta Scott King Illustrator Honor Book)

I Have a Dream (1963)

Amy Littlesugar

Tree of Hope (2001)

Patricia C. McKissack and Frederick L. McKissack Authors of multiple Newbery, Caldecott, ALA, and Coretta Scott King award-winning books

Rebels Against Slavery–American Slave Revolts (1997; Coretta Scott King Author Honor Book)

Ma Dear's Aprons (1997)

Paule Marshall Barbados immigrant storyteller

Praisesong for the Widow (1983)

Brown Girl, Brownstone (1959)

Angela Shelf Medearis Austin, Texas, author

Dancing with the Indians (1991)

Picking Peas for a Penny (1990)

William Miller Author of nonfiction picture books

Richard Wright and the Library Card (1997)

Zora Hurston and the Chinaberry (1994)

Margaret King Mitchell

Uncle Jed's Barbershop (1994; Coretta Scott King Illustrator Honor Book)

Isabell Monk

Hope (2001)

Family (2001)

Toni Morrison Recipient of 1993 Nobel Prize and Pulitzer Prize for fiction

Song of Solomon (1978; National Book Critics Circle Award for fiction)

Sula (1974)

The Bluest Eye (1971)

Beloved (1970)

Walter Dean Myers ALA Lifetime Achievement Award

Bad Boy: A Memoir (2001)

Monster (1999; Coretta Scott King Award)

Amistad: A Long Road to Freedom (1998; IRA Children's Choice)

Slam (1997; Coretta Scott King Honor Book)

The Glory Field (1994)

Now Is Your Time: The African American Struggle for Freedom (1992; Coretta Scott King Author Award)

Scorpions (1989; Newbery Honor Book)

Rosa Parks Mother of twentieth-century Civil Rights Movement

Dear Mrs. Parks (1996)

Andrea Davis Pinkney Author, and **Brian Pinkney** Honored illustrator

Duke Ellington: The Piano Prince (1999)

Alvin Ailey (1993)

Gloria Pinkney

Back Home (1992)

Jerry Pinkney Award-winning illustrator and storyteller

Noah's Ark (2003; Caldecott Honor Book)

Sandra L. Pinkney Author of illustrated books

Faith Ringgold

Aunt Harriet's Underground Railroad in the Sky (1992; Jane Addams Children's Book Award 1993)

Tar Beach (1992; Coretta Scott King Illustrator Award)

Sonia Sanchez Poet and playwright

Homegirls and Handgrenades (1985; American Book Award for poetry)

Kim L. Siegelson First recipient of Center for Multicultural Children's Literature Writing Award

In the Time of the Drums (1999; 2000 Coretta Scott King Award)

Natasha Anastasia Tarpley

I Love My Hair (1998)

Mildred D. Taylor

The Land (2001; 2002 Coretta Scott King Award; Scott O'Dell Award for Historical Fiction; ALA Notable Book; ALA Best Book for Young Adults)

The Road to Memphis (1991; Coretta Scott King Author Award)

The Friendship (1987; 1988 Coretta Scott King Author Award)

Gold Cadillac (1987)

Let the Circle Be Unbroken (1982; Coretta Scott King Author Award)

Song of the Trees (1996; *New York Times* Outstanding Book of the Year)

Roll of Thunder, Hear My Cry (1977; Newbery Medal)

Joyce Carol Thomas Novelist and poet

I Have Heard of a Land (1999; Coretta Scott King Illustrator Honor Book)

Marked by Fire (1999; National Book Award)

Brown Honey in Broomwheat Tea (1993; Coretta Scott King Author and Illustrator Award Book)

Velma Maia Thomas Curator of Black Holocaust Exhibit

Freedom's Children: The Passage from Emancipation to the Great Migration (2000)

Lest We Forget: The Passage from Africa to Slavery and Emancipation (1997)

Jacqueline L. Tobin

Hidden in Plain View: A Secret Story of Quilts and the Underground Railroad (1999)

Alice Walker

Finding the Greenstone (1991)

The Color Purple (1983; Pulitzer Prize, American Book Award)

Booker T. Washington

Up from Slavery (1901)

Phillis Wheatley Author of first poetry book published by an African American

"Liberty and Peace" (1784)

Poems on Various Subjects, Religious and Moral (1773)

"A Poem by Phillis, A Negro Girl, on the Death of Reverend George Whitefield" (1770)

Richard Wright WPA Writer Award and Guggenheim Fellowship recipient

Black Boy (1945; Book-of-the-Month Club Choice)

Native Son (1940; Book-of-the-Month Club Choice)

Sharon Dennis Wyeth

Something Beautiful (1998)

MIND MIXER: BOOK TALK

Begin the school term by establishing a community of storytellers and listeners. Allow students frequent opportunities to talk about books and about reading and writing. Place students in small groups of two to four students. Even numbers work best to avoid having one student feeling left out. For early ages keep simple pairs. Establish firm guidelines for your reading-writing workshop.

- Respect one another.
- Speak softly.
- Care enough to share.

Activity

1. Discuss a favorite childhood story in small group.
2. Discuss a favorite book.
3. After 7 to 10 minutes of small group time, reconvene class.
4. Discuss why people like and need stories.

VOCABULARY

anthropologist	legacy	playwright
covetousness	legendary	poet laureate
curator	literature	posthumous
depository	lithe	publish
dialectical	longevity	pulpous
djeli	lyric	rampant
enlightenment	massive	recipient
esteemed	memoir	regal
griot	notable	renaissance
historian	paradise	respite
inauguration	pauper	rogue
journal	pillar	vanity
journalist	plagued	wavering
landmark		

FOLKLORE

The Baobab Tree
(Senegalese legend)

On the boundless rolling hills of far West Africa, the Matriarch of all trees stands arms extended heavenward. From Barbados to Australia from Madagascar to Vendaland to Senegal, legends and superstitions surrounding this upside down tree thrive. Before God created the ebony, the cedar, the oil palm, the mahogany, the kola nut, the papyrus, the satinwood, the olive, the fig, the mangrove, and the rosewood trees, he planted the beautiful baobab tree in the midst of His garden. Yet, discontent and envy, rogue elephants, ran rampant through Mama Baobab's mind as she looked around at the other trees God created.

"Why am I not lithe and elegant like the palm? Look at me, heavy and awkward as an elephant! Ah, if only I could bend as the breath of God blows my way like Sister Palm!"

Mama Baobab saw the fig tree, clusters of sweet, ripened figs hanging from its branches. A taste of the fig tree's fruit rekindled the fire of dissatisfaction. "My branches are plagued with food fit for baboons while the fruit of the fig tree graces the table of the chosen of God. 'Fruit of life,' they call the pulpous food that hangs from my limbs. Why, it's mere monkey bread! Why does God withhold the best from me?"

Wavering like the shifting wind between self-pity and covetousness, Mama Baobab held on to one certainty. "No one can dispute my superior beauty. I am surely goddess of the savannah. No tree has more splendor than I, with my branches adorned by flowers of richest, royal purple and the purest white." Soothed by her vanity, the ancient of trees took a brief respite from her frivolous complaints until she spotted the startling, scarlet flower blossoms of the flame tree. "My purple blossoms fade like the pauper's cloth compared to Sister Flame. How I wish my flowers glowed like fire!"

Wearied of the ill-tempered, self-absorbed baobab, God reached down from the heavens. He plucked the tree of life from His garden quicker than He had turned night to day and heaved her head first into the red sands of the nation now known as Senegal. From that day the regal blooms of the baobab remain on the tree only twenty-four hours before falling to the ground. The baobab's pillarlike hollowed trunk reminds her of the shallowness that led to her exile from Paradise, and her branches perpetually point toward the Creator she displeased.

Now the ancient Matron Tree of Life finds joy in providing asylum for the hunted, shelter for the homeless, a town hall for those seeking enlightenment, and a landmark for the lost. West Africans and travelers have transformed the massive, hollow trunks of baobabs into prisons, homes, tool sheds, refuges, tombs, and altars. Perhaps the oldest of all trees, the baobab lives for thousands of years, legendary for its longevity.

Senegalese bury the remains of their esteemed griots within the baobab's trunk. Perceived as ugly and awkward, the baobab, Mother of Life, this heritage tree has achieved its own unique magnificence.

▼▼▼▼▼

Reader Response Opportunity

Graphic Organizer

Make a Cycle Graph showing the events of "The Baobab Tree."

Open-Ended Response Opportunity

1. What lessons can the reader learn from the baobab's experience?
2. Write a moral for this legend.
3. Does European, Asian, or Native American oral tradition have any tales about vanity or complaining? Explain.
4. How do you think legends and myths originate?
5. Complete a Folklore Chart for "The Baobab Tree."

SENEGALESE TRADITIONAL FOOD FARE

Cuisine Senegalaise, yassa au poulet, couscous, brochettes, crevettes, banana *glacé, cinq centimes* (five cent cookies), *fromage* Senegalese, and the national dish, *ceebu jen.* The French names testify to the infusion of French influence on Senegalese culture. The Atlantic Ocean provides a steady supply of seafood to this coastal nation. Senegalese have no shortage of lobster, prawns, tuna, carp, sole, and other seafood delicacies although the average family, shrouded in poverty, does not feast on the finer oceanic catches of the day. This Muslim stronghold, home to the peculiar baobab, offers a heart-healthy diet free of pork, with colorful fruits and vegetables: mangoes, sweet potatoes, white potatoes, carrots, eggplant, cabbage, turnips, corn, oranges, bananas, papayas, grapefruits, and lemons. Poor families may enjoy only one daily meal, but the visitor and wealthier resident may enjoy the finest beef, lamb, lobster, prawn, sole, tuna, and exotic seafood not typically found on the American dinner table. George Washington Carver would have found a plentiful supply of groundnuts or peanuts in Senegal to test his many recipes. Small Senegalese children enjoy eating the fruit of Senegal's unique baobab tree. Wash down your *cuisine au Senegal* with ginger, guava, mango, or bissap juice. *Bon appetite.*

Reader Response Opportunity

1. Research Senegalese recipes and eating customs. Suggested Web sites:

   African Studies Cookbook.
   http://www.sas.upenn.edu/African_Studies/Cookbook/cb_spot.html.

   Senegal Cooking.
   http://www.au-senegal.com/art_en/cuisine.htm.

   Congo Cookbook.
   http://www.congocookbook.com/c0202.html.

   The African Guide.
   http://www.africaguide.com/cooking.htm.

2. Research couscous, baobab, and groundnut recipes.

3. Select a recipe or custom.

4. Write a how-to composition about your selection.

5. How do religion, ethnic origin, population, and geographical location affect the eating habits, traditional foods, and dining customs of Senegal? Be specific.

PICTURE BOOK SELECTIONS

To Be a Drum.
Evelyn Coleman. Illustrated by Aminah Lynn Robinson.
Morton Grove, IL: Albert Whitman & Company, 1998.

From the African continent to a new world, this book tells the story of African Americans and how our drum was born. This rhythmic story of courage, survival, and triumph inspires the reader to be a drum.

More Than Anything Else.
Marie Bradby. Illustrated by Chris Soenpiet.
New York: Orchard Books, 1995.

A nine-year-old boy harbors a hunger in his soul for literacy. More than anything else, this son of a salt worker wants to unlock the secrets hidden on the pages of books and in the black marks on newsprint. In his family's cabin by candlelight, the young boy studies a little blue book given to him by his mother and etches the marks on the dirt floor. In the shadow of the lantern's glow, a brown-faced newspaperman teaches the boy to write his name on the ground, B-o-o-k-e-r.

Reader Response Opportunity

1. Booker is excited about learning to read and write. Do young children still feel excited about learning to read? Explain.

2. Think back to your first day of school or your first book (or anything to which you looked forward). Write about your experience.

Zora Hurston and the Chinaberry Tree.
William Miller. Illustrated by Cornelius Van Wright and Ying-Hwa Hu.
New York: Lee & Low Books, 1994.

In the declining years of the nineteenth century, a young child learns to listen to the voices of her people. Living in the earliest, exclusively African American incorporated town, Zora hears the stories carried from old Africa and those first told on American soil. Overcoming the bonds her times placed on young ladies and driven by the tragic death of her mother, a chinaberry tree, and her love of stories bequeathed by her mother, Zora Hurston tells the stories that keep her people alive and writes new stories of her own.

Reader Response Opportunity

Prewriting Strategy

1. Divide a page into three columns.
2. In the first column, list all that Zora learns from her father.
3. In the second column, list all that she learns from her mother.
4. In the third column, list all that she learns at the campfires.

Graphic Organizer

Make a Bio Graph of Zora's life.

Open-Ended Response Opportunity

1. What does the Chinaberry represent to Zora?
2. Give two examples of figurative language from the book. Identify each as a simile, metaphor, personification, or hyperbole.
3. Does Zora keep the promises she made to her mother? Explain.

Coming Home: From the Life of Langston Hughes.
Written and illustrated by Floyd Cooper.
New York: Philomel Books, 1994.

ALA Notable Book.

Deferred dreams drive young Langston's life—dreams of freedom fought for by his grandma's first husband, a freedom fighter with John Brown, dreams of honor by his Buffalo Soldier uncles, and dreams of a home with his father and mother struggling in their own careers. Shuffled from Granma to Mama to Daddy to friends of the family, James Langston Hughes realizes his dreams and finds his home in the music and lives of common people.

Reader Response Opportunity

Graphic Organizer

Make a timeline of Langston's childhood.

Open-Ended Response Opportunity

1. The author describes Langston's home as "a blues song in the pale evening night." In what ways is Langston's home life as a child a blues song?

2. In spite of the life Langston Hughes experienced, he penned poems that inspired people who had come through hopeless circumstances. Authors such as Maya Angelou and Lorraine Hansberry have used poignant phrases from poetry by Langston Hughes as titles for their own writings, *I Know Why the Caged Bird Sings* and *A Raisin in the Sun*. Read some poetry by Langston Hughes and write your reflections in your log.

Richard Wright and the Library Card.
William Miller.
New York: Lee & Low Books, 1997.

Smithsonian Notable Children's Book.
Society of School Librarians International Honor Book.

Born of hard-working laborers in Jim Crow Mississippi, young Richard yearns for a ticket to a better life. In Memphis the furtive support of a man for whom he works gives Richard his entrance to shelves stacked with the works of Charles Dickens, Leo Tolstoy, Stephen Crane, and others. Words, ideas, and histories forever change Richard Wright.

Reader Response Opportunity

Graphic Organizer

Make a Ring Graph of the events that allow Richard Wright to check books out from the library.

Open-Ended Response Opportunity

1. What in his childhood makes words and stories important to Richard?

2. In what ways is the library card a ticket to freedom?

NONFICTION SELECTIONS

Bad Boy: A Memoir.
Walter Dean Myers.
New York: HarperCollins, 2001.

Strong, angry, restless, and bright, Walter reads and analyzes books with an obsession, but the classroom holds no appeal for him. A superior body of young adult literature that has won numerous prestigious awards attests to Walter Dean Myers' success in creating stories to feed other bright minds.

Reader Response Opportunity

Graphic Organizer

Make a Bio Graph of Walter's life.

Open-Ended Response Opportunity

1. Do you think *Bad Boy* is an appropriate title for Walter Dean's memoirs? Explain.
2. Do you think many restless and disruptive students are like Walter, not challenged?
3. If you were one of Walter's teachers, what would you do to make him want to be at school?

Up from Slavery.
Booker T. Washington.
New York: Dover Publications, 1995. (First Published by Doubleday, Page and Company, 1901).

This chronological collection of essays about experiences in the life of Booker T. Washington, a former slave and a respected educator and leader, is worth reading to examine the views of the predominant African American of his time. Suggested readings from the book include:

Chapter I: "A Slave among Slaves," relates the slave experience from a child's perspective in the waning days of slavery's dominance.

Chapter V: "The Reconstruction Period," gives Washington's impression of the years from 1867 through 1878. He shares his unflattering views of "coloured" preachers, teachers, and carpetbaggers.

Reader Response Opportunity

Graphic Organizer

Make a Venn diagram comparing and contrasting Washington and any other prominent African American leader and spokesperson, for example, W. E. B. Du Bois or Dr. Martin Luther King, Jr.

Short-Answer Response Opportunity

Booker T. Washington states, "No one section of our country was wholly responsible for its [Slavery's] introduction, and, besides, it was recognized and protected for years by the General

Government" (8). Do you believe the North shares responsibility with the South for slavery's long regime in this country? Why?

Debate

Write and/or act out a debate between W. E. B. Du Bois and the leader you chose for your T-chart, reflecting their principal ideas and highlighting their differences.

To Be Young, Gifted and Black: An Informal Autobiography of Lorraine Hansberry.
Lorraine Hansberry. Adapted by Robert Nemiroff. Introduction by James Baldwin.
New York: Signet Books, 1969.

This unconventional autobiography attempts to capture the essence of Lorraine Hansberry, from gleanings of her writings, speeches, letters, journals, and interviews. Complete with photographs of Ms. Hansberry and fan letters to her, *To Be Young, Gifted and Black* presents an enigmatic, truly gifted woman with generous portions of pride, anger, fear, and foresight.

Reader Response Opportunity

1. Write five or more questions you would like to ask Ms. Hansberry.
2. Read the correspondence in the autobiography. Write a letter to Ms. Hansberry about something specific she says.

Black Boy.
Richard Wright.
New York: HarperCollins, 1945.

Book-of-the-Month Club Selection.

Black Boy chronicles the life of Mississippi-born Wright and his clashes with racial prejudice and injustice.

Reader Response Opportunity

Prewriting/Graphic Organizer

Make a timeline or Bio Graph of pivotal events in Wright's life.

Open-Ended Response Opportunity

1. What do the events of the writer's life reveal about the way of life and racial relationships in America at the time?
2. In your opinion, have racial relationships changed since that time? Explain.

I Know Why the Caged Bird Sings.
Maya Angelou.
New York: Random House, 1969.

In the first volume of her personal narrative, Maya Angelou, uncaged, tells a stirring story of the anguish of growing up as an African American girl in the American South. Ms. Angelou's life story, candid and free of bitterness and judgment, soars like the skylark's flight song, lingering long after the bird is out of sight.

Heart of a Woman.
Maya Angelou.
New York: Random House, 1981.

Ms. Angelou recounts first-hand experiences with notable people, places, and organizations in twentieth-century African American life: Billie Holiday, Dr. Martin Luther King, Jr., the Apollo Theater, the Southern Christian Leadership Conference, the Harlem Writers Guild, Paule Marshall, Godfrey Cambridge, Harry Belafonte, and Sidney Poitier. Maya Angelou's words flow slow and easy on the printed page, like honey, telling an intriguing story not only of Maya Angelou, but also of Black and White America in transition in its second millennia.

A Song Flung Up to Heaven.
Maya Angelou.
New York: Random House, 2002.

Only Maya Angelou could write four autobiographies and continue to enthrall and inspire her readers. Ms. Angelou has lived a sweet and sour life. Tragedy cuts into Maya Angelou's life regularly leaving its scars, while historical figures who have graced the covers and pages of *Time, Newsweek,* and *Ebony* walk in and out of her home and life, seeking counsel and support. Yet, she makes time to embrace her family and friends. Her life is a song flung up to Heaven.

Reader Response Opportunity

Graphic Organizer

Make a web showing all the important people Ms. Angelou encountered while in New York.

Open-Ended Response Opportunity

As an entertainer and writer, Ms. Angelou became active in the Civil Rights Movement.

1. Is it important for famous people to take an active role in politics? Why?
2. What examples of this do we see in current events? Explain?
3. From her writings explain what is important to the heart of the woman, Maya Angelou?

Black Stars: African American Women Writers.
Brenda Wilkinson. General editor, Jim Haskins.
New York: John Wiley & Sons, 2000.

Refined by the fire of sexual and racial oppression and beaten into form by the burdens of African American womanhood, the writers have emerged as pure gold. Phillis Wheatley wrote of the inherent love of freedom. Sojourner Truth asked, "Ain't I a woman?" Harriet Jacobs alerted the nation of the ravage of enslaved women with her *Incidents in the Life of a Slave Girl* (1861). These Mother Eve's of African American storytellers have fulfilled the honored role of generations of djelis, preserving our history and heritage. This encyclopedia of three centuries of chroniclers also lists additional authors and a timeline.

Reader Response Opportunity

1. Select an author from the *Black Stars* or from the list in this chapter.

2. Write a profile on your selected author in the form of an obituary, a who's who, a nomination for an award, or any other creative format. Select at least one work of the storyteller to review in your profile.

WRITING PROMPTS

Elementary Writing Prompt

Around the world, people of all ages enjoy telling and listening to stories.
Parents read nursery rhymes and fairy tales to their young children. Both children and grownups seem to love hearing and telling stories.

Write about the importance of stories.

Secondary Writing Prompt

Africa, like every continent and culture, has a strong oral tradition, but it does not have a particularly full vault of written literature dating back to before the twentieth century.

Does oral tradition have a positive impact on written literature?

Multilevel Writing Prompt

Richard Wright circumvented unjust restrictions to obtain a library card. Not every society has a public library system.

Write about the importance of free, public libraries.

B
▼▼▼▼▼

Over Jordan: Ancestral Africa

Do not call the forest that shelters you a jungle.
—Ashanti proverb

Deep River

Deep river, my home is over Jordan.
Deep river, I want to cross over into campground.
Deep river, my home is over Jordan.
Deep river, I want to cross over into campground.

O, don't you want to go to that gospel feast,
That promised land where all is peace?
Deep river, my home is over Jordan.
Deep river, I want to cross over into campground.

HISTORICAL CONTEXT

Africa, a continent rich with natural resources: lush grasslands, exotic animals, diamonds, gold; Africa, kings, kingdoms, mighty warriors, civilization's birthplace; Africa, etymologists debate the history of this vast continent's name. Africa, originally this Greco-Roman word denoted sunshine and warmth and first applied to the northern regions of the continent. Africa, attitudes toward this continent have frequently been obscured by prejudice, ignorance, shame, and tradition and chilled by brutality, greed, and betrayal. In times past, literature, the media, historians, and archaeologists have oftentimes misrepresented it as a dark, savage land with no more to offer than jungles overflowing with primates, elephants, zebras, giraffes, Tarzan, lions, other wild animals, and uncivilized, unclothed natives. Africa, old as time, a colossal baobab, its roots, torn from the soil, reach outward and upward, hosts fifty-three nations and hides the secrets to humanity's genesis in its bosom.

Early historians and archaeologists attributed the great achievements of Africa to Arabian, Asian, or other non-African sources. Many outsiders condescended to acknowledge the magnificence of the Egyptian civilization but could not accept the possibility that indigenous Africans created the marvels of these ancient civilizations. Conventional thinking often ignored or downplayed the triumphs and virtues of Africa's people. The need for slave labor in the New World led to the perpetuation of the time-honored European and Western notion of the Black African as a soulless, primitive savage. Accepted European and Western thought perceived black and brown Africans as not possessing the intellect to build great edifices, mine gold, or organize and regulate intricate political and military systems. Archaeologists ascribed the ruins of Great Zimbabwe and the Meroë Pyramid of the Nubian or Kush civilization to the intervention of Indian, Egyptian, or Arab cultures. Apocryphal information and tradition has led many around the world to believe nothing of value came from sub-Saharan Africa.

On the contrary, Africa is the forest that shelters the roots of humanity's family tree. African soil may well qualify as the fertile womb that conceived and nurtured our prehistoric predecessors. Based on human ancestral fossil findings, paleontologists hypothesize that early humans took their first fully upright, two-legged steps on the African continent less than two million years ago. Primitive humans in their infancy most likely breathed their initial breath of life and took their earliest, toddling, baby steps on the land that produced the extraordinary Egyptian empire. Sundiata, the original Lion King of Mali, the pharaohs, Askia the Great, Olaudah Equiano, and the ancestors of history-making Americans like Crispus Attucks, Phillis Wheatley, Frederick Douglass, W. E. B. Du Bois, Booker T. Washington, Dr. Charles Drew, Thurgood Marshall, Julian Bond, Dr. Martin Luther King, Coretta Scott King, Medgar Evans, Barbara Jordan, Shirley Chisholm, and Colin Powell almost certainly hunted, farmed, fished, ate, slept, loved, and raised children on the continent first inhabited by creation's first man and woman.

In Genesis 2:13, the Bible's book of beginnings, Moses refers to Ethiopia, or Cush, encompassed by the Tigris River when he describes the four waterways flowing from Adam and Eve's lost paradise, the Garden of Eden (KJV). The Greek poet Homer praises Nubia in his epic poetry. The Bible contains tens of references to Aethiopia (Ethiopia, ancient name for the African continent). Not only is Africa the ancestral home of Black African Americans, but there is also mounting evidence verifying Africa as humanity's Bethlehem stable.

Across the African continent, second only to Asia in size and population, flows the world's longest river, the Nile. Mount Kilimanjaro, the dormant volcano immortalized by Ernest Hemingway, reaches into the clouds at an altitude of nearly 20,000 feet. Africa additionally boasts the Sahara Desert. Cutting through Arabia and Northeast Africa, the Red Sea parted at the outstretched hand of Moses to allow the Israelites to flee from the Egyptian army. Beginning in the early 600s B.C., Muslims from the Middle East crossed into Egypt. In the 1400s and 1500s Portugal and subsequent European nations navigated the seas to explore and exploit the wealth of Africa: its gold, ivory, copper, diamonds, iron, and ebony flesh. Thirteen percent of the world's population lives in the fifty-three independent nations of Africa. Africa's cultural diversity rivals that of the United States, with more than 1,000 languages spoken and numerous ethnic groups, including Arabs, Black Africans, Dutch, English, Christians, Jews, Muslims, Buddhists, Taoists, and Hindus. By the year 2050 African inhabitants will represent twenty percent of the world's population.

People skilled in crafts, art, architecture, agriculture, irrigation, and the oral tradition developed kingdoms, mined gold and diamonds, and constructed magnificent edifices. Pharaohs, Asantehenes (Ashanti kings), Obas, chiefs, kings, queens, emirs, and councils of elders ruled the many people of Africa. Egypt headlines the list of well-known, great, ancient, African civilizations, followed by lesser known kingdoms and empires: the Kush (Nubia), Axsum (present-day Ethiopia), Luba, and the Kongo (Congo) Kingdoms, the Mwanamutapa, and the Changamire Empires. Counted among West African notable kingdoms are the ancient Ghana Kingdom, the Ashanti (Asante), the Baganda Kingdom, the Bénin, and Hausa Kingdoms, the Mali Empire, and the Songhay (Songhai) Empire. Egyptians, Kushites or Cushites, Soninkes, Mandinkas, Songhays, Bushmen of South Central Africa, the Mende, and other tribes, city-states, and kingdoms conducted their daily lives until Portuguese traders trailed by other Europeans identified a resource more valuable in building the New World than ivory and gold: black flesh. "New World Slavery" changed the rhythm of human history and continues to have impact on both the African and North American continents.

MIND MIXER: BRAINSTORMING

Brainstorming aptly describes the whirlwind of ideas generated in the synergetic atmosphere of a safe, literate, interactive classroom environment. Accept all contributions; reject none. Focus on bringing ideas out into the open and stimulating thought.

1. Have students, in groups of 2 to 4, brainstorm everything that comes to their minds when they hear the word Africa.
2. Have a spokesperson record the group's answers.
3. After 10 minutes, let the spokesperson for each group share its results.
4. Record the answers on the overhead transparency, on butcher paper, on a chart tablet, or on the board.
5. Have a whole group discussion about the trends seen in the answers given.

VOCABULARY

Akan	baobab	culture
ancestor	biblical	Cushite/Kushite
ancestral	civilization	custom
Ananse/Anansi	coffers	descendant
Ashanti	continent	emir
asset	cowry	empire

ethnic	Kiswahili	primitive
etymologist	maize	regalia
exotic	nation	resource
generation	Nubia/Nubian	sub-Saharan
Greco-Roman	paleontologist	superstition
Hausa	Pan-African	Swahili
heir	population	tribal
indigenous	predecessor	Twi
inhabitants	prehistoric	weaponry
kingdom	primate	

FOLKLORE

This creation tale reflects Yoruba mythology. With a plot as old as Cain and Abel and recurrent as Jacob and Esau, a father with two sons enjoys the blessing of an heir who hastens to please his father and the curse of a rash, thankless child whose path leads to destruction. Variations of the following Yoruba creation myth present Oduduwa, or Odudua, as the obedient son who creates earth and Obatala as the drunken ne're-do-well who fails to fulfill his father's wishes. The place where Oduduwa, heir to the ruler of earth and sky, first forms land becomes Yoruba's sacred city, Ile Ifa. So, sit down and hear the story of a father, his sons, and a new land, Yorubaland.

The Beginning of Beginnings
(Retelling of a Nigerian Yoruba myth)

▼▼▼▼▼

In the beginning of all beginnings, only water lay beneath the skies. Olorun, ruler of earth and sky, desired a foundation on the earth below to allow his two sons to walk the earth and rule over it. Accordingly, Olorun dropped a seedling palm tree from the sky. Oh, so quickly the palm tree grew, reaching its branches upward toward the sky and stretching them wide as a mother's arms waiting to embrace her child. After the tree grew to its fullness, Olorun called his two sons, Oduduwa and Obatala, to his side.

"Sons, look below. All that you see will be yours. Take this bag; it holds all you will need to create land. Then I will let down the golden cord and lower you to the branches of the palm tree. Behave prudently, my sons. You have only this one chance to change the water into soil. On this land your people will plant trees, grow food, build huts, hunt animals, dance, and play, all for your pleasure. Are you ready to go below?"

"Yes, Father," Oduduwa promptly agreed.

Obatala, shiftless as the least of all hyenas, gave the chief no answer but unenthusiastically followed his brother, Oduduwa, to the golden cord. Olorun bid his sons farewell and sent them down to earth. As soon as foolish Obatala reached the palm tree's branches, he tapped the tree for its wine, made himself drunk, and fell to the bottom of the tree. Little by little water covered his face. To this day irresponsible Obatala lives beneath the waters.

Faithful to his task, Oduduwa climbed down to the bottom of the palm tree and examined the bag his father had given him. In the bag he found sand white as salt, black soil, a chameleon, and a hen. He reached into the bag, took out handfuls of the white sand, and scattered it over the face of the water. Then he set the chameleon down to test the surface of the water. Seeing that the earth still needed firmness, Oduduwa emptied the black soil from the bag onto the ground, set the hen on the soil, and watched as the hen scratched the ground, spreading the fertile soil across the land.

In Obatala's watery domain, fish, crocodile, and other creatures swam; hippotamuses bathed. On the fertile soil, Oduduwa cultivated maize given to him by his father, Olorun, and grew other crops to feed his people. Dense tropical forests of rubber trees, palm trees, walnut trees, mahogany, and eucalyptus provided a haven for the varied collection of wild animals who roamed freely: elephants, baboons, gorillas, lions, monkeys, leopards, zebras, elands, vultures, and cheetahs. The earth, pregnant with promise, flourished.

Pleased with his eldest son's wisdom and obedience, Olorun proclaimed Oduduwa first ruler of Yorubaland. He sent Oduduwa additional gifts, cowries and bars of iron, as a sign of his pleasure. Best of all, Olorun presented his son with a wife. Oduduwa and his wife enjoyed a fine life ruling Yorubaland. They drank of the palm wine, ate the maize they had planted, used the palm tree's oil for cooking, adorned themselves with necklaces and bracelets from the cowries, and formed tools to hunt, skin animals, fish, and defend their land. Oduduwa's wife gave birth to robust sons and daughters whose skin was the dusky hue of baobab tree bark and who presented them with many grandchildren, great grandchildren, and great great grandchildren. You might say Oduduwa is the ancient grandfather of the grandfathers I never knew. This is the story of the beginning of beginnings.

Reader Response Opportunity

Prewriting Strategy

1. Discuss with the students the characteristics of oral tradition.
2. Introduce students to the Folklore Chart by completing one with the whole class on "The Baobab Tree" (see Chapter 2).
3. Have students complete a Folklore Chart on "The Beginning of Beginnings." Primary children can draw a picture and talk about their drawing with a partner or the teacher.
4. Make a Venn diagram to compare and contrast the two sons.

Open-Ended Response Opportunity

1. How does this Yoruba creation myth compare to the other theories or beliefs about how the world was formed?
2. Is this creation myth similar to any other folktales or myths you have read or heard? Explain.
3. Why do you think people around the world, throughout history, have their own variation of the creation story?

Creation Stories Research

1. Research the Genesis creation account or a Greek, Roman, Norse, or Native American creation myth.

Suggested book:

> *In the Beginning: Creation Stories from Around the World.*
> Virginia Hamilton. Illustrated by Barry Moser.
> San Diego, CA: Harcourt Brace Jovanovich, 1988

2. Make a T-chart showing the similarities and differences between the Yoruba myth and another version of the foundation of the earth.

3. Write a composition comparing and contrasting the Yoruba creation myth to another story of creation.

TRADITIONAL PALM TREE FOOD FARE

The African palm tree grows freely in the tropical regions of Africa, providing a source of income and food. Workers extract palm oil from the fruit of African palm trees to use not only as a cooking oil for meats, vegetables, and seafood, but also as a distinct ingredient in palm butter, sauces, stews, and soups. Additionally, African cooks make use of palm nuts in stews and use palm sap to create wine.

Reader Response Opportunity

1. Research the process of making palm oil. Suggested Web sites:

   http://www.congocookbook.com.
   (Search: *Congo Cookbook*)

   http://www.sas.upenn.edu/African_Studies/Miscellany/Recipes.
   (search: *Miscellany recipes*)

2. Make a Cycle Graph showing how palm oil is made.

3. Find a recipe that uses palm oil or any other palm product.

4. Write an explanatory composition telling how to make a dish using a palm tree product.

PICTURE BOOK SELECTIONS

Ashanti to Zulu: African Traditions.
Margaret Musgrove. Pictures by Leo and Diane Dillon.
New York: The Dial Press, 1976.

Caldecott Medal.

Ashanti to Zulu: African Traditions commences with the Ashanti's *kente* cloth and concludes with the Zulu's goatskin leg bands and armbands. This artistic delight offers vivid, captivating illustrations of twenty-six African tribes and their distinctive customs.

Jambo Means Hello.
Muriel Feelings. Illustrated by Tom Feelings.
New York: Dial Books for Young Readers, 1971.

Caldecott Honor Book; ALA Notable Book;
Boston Globe/Horn Book Award for Illustration.

From *arusi* to *zeze, Jambo Means Hello,* a forerunner in African alphabet books, introduces the twenty-four letter Kiswahili alphabet. The strength and nobility of the depicted people reach out from Tom Feelings' black-and-white sketches. The reader will be tempted to trace the wrinkles mapping the elder's face and touch the white beard, like sheep's wool, on the medicine man.

A Is for Africa.
Written and photographed by Ifeoma Onyefulu.
United Kingdom: Puffin Books, 1997.

Notable Children's Trade Book; American Booksellers Association "Pick of the Lists."

A Is for Africa pairs the author's photographs of Nigeria with interesting tidbits about village life in the West African nation. (*Objet trouve:* Die cut-out of a letter of the alphabet or alphabet cereal)

Africa Dream.
Eloise Greenfield. Illustrated by Carole Byard.
New York: HarperCollins, 1977.

Coretta Scott King Award, 1978.

A little girl's Africa dream transports her to "long-ago Africa." The author's lyrical phrases matched with ethereal black-and-white images take the reader sleepwalking though quiet villages.

Reader Response Opportunity

Prewriting Strategy

1. Make a web showing everything the young girl sees and does in "long-ago Africa." (Primary/ Elementary)
2. Make a web showing all the images created by the dreamer in *Africa Dream.* (Secondary/ Post-Secondary)

Open-Ended Response Opportunity

(Primary/Elementary)

1. Does the girl in *Africa Dream* enjoy her dream-visit to Africa? How can you tell?
2. Why do you think the girl wants to go to Africa?
3. Have you ever wanted to visit a place or always wondered about a place and finally gotten to visit it?

(Secondary/Post-Secondary)

1. Do you think it is important for a person to know about his/her background? Why?
2. If you could visit one place to learn more about your family's heritage, where would you choose? Explain.

Kofi and His Magic.
Maya Angelou.
Photography by Margaret Courtney-Clarke.
New York: Clarkson Potter, 1996.

With words woven as expertly as royal *kente* cloth, Maya Angelou portrays a young boy's pride in his Ghanaian home. Kofi's love hints at Ms. Angelou's bond with the West Africa of her personal pilgrimage. With the enthusiasm and openness of a carefree child, Kofi, Friday's child, welcomes the reader to explore his magical world. (*Objet trouve:* two- to four-inch square of *kente* cloth or other African cloth)

Reader Response Opportunity

Graphic Organizer

Make a Venn diagram that compares the images and experiences of West Africa in *Kofi's Magic* and *Africa Dream*.

Open-Ended Response Opportunity

1. Kofi believes he lives in the most beautiful place in the world. In what ways is his town special?
2. What makes your hometown or favorite place special? Give specific details.
3. Why does Kofi believe he is magical?
4. Are there any ways in which you feel magical? Explain.
5. Both Kofi and the narrator in *Africa Dream* let their imaginations take them to another time and place. Which author would you choose to accompany on a journey? Why?

Research

1. Research traditional Twi names. Find out the Twi name you would have based on the day of the week you were born. Suggested site:

    Your Name in Twi.
    http://www.fiankoma.org/schoolsite/yourname.htm.
2. Research African cloth: *kente* cloth, mud cloth, or proverb cloth.
    Briefly describe the cloth and outline its history and meaning. If your hometown or state were to have a special cloth that represented it, what would it look like? Explain.

A Country Far Away.
Nigel Gray. Illustrated by Philippe Dupasquier
New York: Orchard Books, 1998.

Parents Magazine Best Books of the Year.

In straightforward narrative text and drawings, *A Country Far Away* skillfully showcases the common experiences of children. Two boys, one in Africa and one in Europe, describe their ordinary days. The text affirms the commonalities of happy childhoods, regardless of ethnic, national, cultural, or racial differences, and it illustrates the diverse ways people go about their "ordinary day." (*Objet trouve:* mini globe)

Reader Response Opportunity

Prewriting

1. List the events of the boys' lives.
2. Make a T-chart or Venn diagram showing how different the same activity is in each boy's life.

Reader Response Opportunity

1. What is the theme of *A Country Far Away?* Explain.
2. What generalizations can you make from this book? Explain.

Pair Project

1. Pair with a student of a different family background, different interests, or different ethnic group.
2. With a partner, create a comic book or children's picture book about an ordinary day in your life.
3. Use simple text with lively action verbs and vivid images.
4. Illustrate your book with original illustrations, clip art, or magazine cutouts.

Step One (Individual Task) Create a timeline of a typical day in your life. Write a sentence describing each event on your timeline and illustrate your timeline.

Step Two (Paired Task) Pair off and discuss timelines with a partner. Use the following guide questions with your partner:

  • What does a typical day look like in your life?

  • Who wakes you up in the mornings?

  • What do meal times look like? Does everyone sit down to eat together?

  • How does your family celebrate?

Step Three Partners select shared sentences to put in your book. Proofread your sentences for subject-verb agreement, punctuation, capitalization, and correct sentence structure.

Step Four Collaborate with your partner to create your book. Share your book with the class.

Sundiata: Lion King of Mali.
Written and illustrated by David Wisniewski.
New York: Clarion Books, 1992.

In the captivating style of fairy tales and folktales from around the world, the retelling of the legend of Sundiata, King of Mali, presents the underdog, a handicapped, disenfranchised royal heir, and his ultimate triumph over his enemies. Treachery, sorcery, and intrigue color this tale about the handicapped, exiled heir to the Mali Empire. As with all quality oral tradition, righteousness defeats evil for a happily ever after ending. (*Objet trouve*: lion)

Reader Response Opportunity

Discussion

Discuss the legend of Sundiata.

Graphic Organizer

Make a Bio Graph of Sundiata's life.

Open-Ended Response Opportunity

1. What lessons can the reader learn from Sundiata's life?
2. What other characters, real or fictional, overcame substantial obstacles in life to achieve their goals? Discuss.

The Dancing Granny
Written and illustrated by Ashley Bryan.
New York: Aladdin Paperbacks, 1977.

Ashley Bryan's words and illustrations dance and swing across each page. Granny Anika sings, drums, claps, slaps, and dances her way through her day as she stirs her pot of stew and plants seeds of potatoes, corn, peas, and beans. Brother Ananse, master trickster and slacker, sings Granny's feet happy as he tries to wile away her vegetables. Ultimately, Granny gets the best of Brother Ananse. (*Objet trouve:* spider, peas, or beans)

Reader Response Opportunity

Graphic Organizer

Complete a Cycle Graph for *The Dancing Granny*.

Open-Ended Response Opportunity

1. List and give examples of the poetic devices used in *The Dancing Granny*.
2. What does Ashley Bryan do to make the reader feel like dancing?

NONFICTION SELECTIONS

Africa Is Not a Country.
Mary Burns Knight. Illustrated by Anne Sibley O'Brien.
New York: Millbrook Press, 2000.

This reference, geared to intermediate readers, contains a wealth of information about the complex continent of Africa and its fifty-three independent nations. The title and the information within it dispel the mistaken notion of Africa as one simple country rather than a massive, diverse continent inhabited by numerous ethnic groups.

Reader Response Opportunity

Graphic Organizer

Before reading the book, begin a KWL chart, filling in what you know in the K column and what you want to know in the W column. After reading the book, complete the L column with what you learned. Then place a star or check by at least one topic in the W column about which you still want to know more.

Open-Ended Response Opportunity

1. In your opinion, is Africa an important continent? Explain.
2. Each part of the world offers valuable resources. In your opinion, what is the most valuable resource Africa has given the world? Support your choice with specific facts.

Research

1. Research any one of the fifty-three African nations.
2. Create a fact/profile sheet about the nation that includes the following:
    - Background on the country's name
    - Geographical location
    - Early civilizations of the country
    - Ethnic groups
    - Languages spoken
    - Religions
    - Colonial rule
    - Information about the independence of the nation
    - Resources
    - Interesting trivia

African Beginnings.
James Haskins and Kathleen Benson. Illustrated by Floyd Cooper.
New York: Lothrop, Lee, & Shepard, 1998.

The first volume of a seven-part series on Africa, *African Beginnings* chronicles Africa from its infancy in 3800 B.C. until the advent of the European slave trade. With expressive exposition and earthy paintings in deep browns, sunburst oranges, regal purples, and majestic blues, the African story unfolds.

Reader Response Opportunity

Graphic Organizer

Make a timeline showing the main time periods in ancient African history.

Research

1. Select a topic from the areas listed below.
2. Create a visual representation: a postcard, travel brochure, advertisement, PowerPoint presentation, Web page, mural, mobile, diorama, political cartoon, etc.
3. Include descriptive/explanatory text with your visual.

Cultures and Kingdoms	*Geographical Locations*
Ancient Ghana	Great Zimbabwe Ruins
Ashanti Kingdom	Meroë Pyramid
Bénin	Mount Kilimanjaro
Hausa Kingdom	Red Sea
Mali Empire	River Nile
Songhai Empire	Sahara Desert

Wonders of the African World.
Henry Louis Gates, Jr. Photography by Lynn Davis.
New York: Alfred A. Knopf, 1999.

Gates accomplishes considerably more than just exploring and revealing the marvels of the African continent. He examines conflicting attitudes about Africa since Europeans first explored it. He puts into question African Americans' ambivalent feelings toward Africa and the Africans who avoided the European slave traders grasp and, who in some cases, acted as co-conspirators by selling their cousins into a cruel fate. This epic handling of Africa's story, its land, history, and people, complements the PBS video series of the same title.'

Reader Response Opportunity

1. Select one of the following topics.
2. Narrow the topic down to a specific aspect with which you want to deal.
3. Write an essay explaining what you learned.
4. Create a visual representation or mini-project reflecting your learning.

- Marcus Garvey
- The Pan-American movement
- The African Union Society of Newport, Rhode Island
- Kedane Mehret
- Fasil's/Fasilda's Castle
- Tabot
- The Twin Churches of Bet Golgota and Bet Debra Sina
- Debra Damo Monastery Stelae of Axum
- St. Mary's Church of Axum
- Konboro Palace
- The School of Three Doors
- Timbuktu
- The Sankoré Mosque
- Bao (A Pan-African Game)
- Tippu Tip
- Sui Generis
- Kwame Nkrumah
- Elmina Castle
- The Gate of Tears
- Nana Obiri Yeboa

All God's Children Got Traveling Shoes.
Maya Angelou.
New York: Vintage Books, 1986.

In her liquid, honest style Maya Angelou tells of her journey to Ghana with her son, Guy, peppered with unexpected tragedy and soul-seeking encounters. Seeing Africa through the eyes of this gifted, insightful African American woman makes the reader thirst to travel there as well.

Reader Response Opportunity

1. How does Maya Angelou's stay in Ghana affect her?

2. Does Maya Angelou learn any lessons while in Ghana? If so, what does she learn?

3. Maya Angelou writes, "The ache for home lives in all of us, the safe place where we can go and not be questioned" (196). What place do you think she decides is her home? How does she show that? What is your safe place or your home? How do you get there?

MULTIMEDIA

Sierra Leone Web.
http://www.sierra-leone.org/freetown1848.htm.

This Web site offers maps, fact sheets, and photographs of the West African nation of Sierra Leone from which the forebears of many African Americans came as slaves.

Reader Response Opportunity

1. How is Sierra Leone similar to your hometown, state, or the U.S.?

2. What does the Web site tell you about the people of Sierra Leone?

3. For many Africans transported across the Atlantic Ocean by European invaders, the sea coast of Sierra Leone served as their point of departure. Today thousands of descendants of freed slaves live in Sierra Leone. Write questions you would ask a Sierra Leone descendant of freedmen.

Ancient Africa (Video).
Schlessinger Media, 1998.

This 23-minute educational video approaches young children at their level by giving them a glimpse of some of the wonders of the African continent. Part of a nine volume series on *Ancient Civilizations for Children,* the video comes with a teacher's guide that includes vocabulary, questions, activities, and suggestions.

Reader Response Opportunity

In your opinion, which civilization was greater, the Swahili or the Great Zimbabwe? Support your choice with specific details from the video.

Ghana, Land of the Gold Coast (Video).
Educational Video, 1999.

This 43-minute video showcases the assets of West Africa's Ghana, which has embraced African Americans in search of their native home.

Open-Ended Response Opportunity

1. How is Ghana similar to the United States?
2. Is Ghana similar to or different from what you expected?

Mini-Research Project

Students will use what they have learned about Africa and write:

- A travel brochure for any part of Africa
- A journal entry as if they are a traveler in Africa
- A journal entry as a resident of an African country/villages
- A newspaper article about an event in Africa.

WRITING PROMPTS

Elementary Writing Prompt

The girl in *Africa Dream* and the boy in *Kofi and His Magic* both describe imaginary journeys to places important to them.

> Write about a journey to an important place.
> What would you see, hear, feel, experience?

Secondary Writing Prompt

Many times people have incomplete or incorrect information about someone or some place, just as many of us have had some misconceptions about Africa. Once we learn more, we often get a completely different idea about the person or place.

> Write about the consequences of believing stereotypes.

Multilevel Writing Prompt 1

Ghanaian tradition has many children named for the day they were born. Kofi of *Kofi and His Magic* is Friday's child.

> Write about the importance of a person's name.

Multilevel Writing Prompt 2

From the moment slavers first forced men and women aboard slave ships and brought them to the shores of North America, Africans in America yearned to return home. Over the course of the history of the United States, the hearts of some African Americans long for a homeland they have never known.

> Write about what makes a place "home."

4
▼▼▼▼▼

Pilgrims of Sorrow: Atlantic Slave Trade

Sorrow is a precious treasure, shown only to friends.
—Kenyan proverb

City Called Heaven

I am a poor pilgrim of sorrow.
I'm lost in this wide world alone.
No hope have I for tomorrow.
I've started to make Heaven my home.

Sometimes I am tossed and I'm driven, Lord.
Sometimes I just don't know where to roam.
I've heard of a city called Heaven.
I've started to make Heaven my home.

My mother has reached that pure glory.
My father is still walking in sin.
My brothers and sisters don't own me.
I'm trying to make it on in.

Sometimes I am tossed and I'm driven, Lord.
Sometimes I just don't know where to roam.
I've heard of a city called Heaven.
I've started to make Heaven my home.

HISTORICAL CONTEXT

Scattered like myriad ripened, feathery seeds from the white-haired crown of an aged dande-lion, pilgrims of sorrow—fathers out seeking food for their children, adolescent girls gathering firewood, young boys fishing, wives collecting water for their families—disappeared from their homes and lives without a trace. Children made up one of every ten of those seized. The families received no ransom notes. No posters, flyers, or milk cartons bore their images. No Missing Persons Bureau sought after them. The ill-fated captives endured forced marches to slave dungeons at the coast. Upon reaching the slave holding pens, slavers shaved the heads of their victims, stripped them of all clothing, and branded them with hot iron or silver. The time of confinement could extend to one full year. The harsh treatment of the captives during their detainment was but a portent of the horrors awaiting them aboard the great sailing vessels.

Chained together in the bellies of slave ships, only the heartiest of the captives survived the cruel journey. Shelved beneath and between the decks, Africans bound for the New World had insufficient space to turn over, less than two feet of head room. During the unrelenting voyage, the stench of human waste, perspiration, blood, tears, despair, and fear permeated the air below deck. Hundreds of kidnapped mothers and fathers, husbands, sons, brothers, wives, sisters, and daughters lived or died at the whim of bands of twenty-five to thirty intruders from across the deep waters of the Atlantic Ocean. Men speaking in strange tongues barked out commands. The terrified prisoners, guilty only of the crime of coarse hair, full lips, and an excess of melanin, received only one or two "African meals" a day of grain, yams, and beans from communal slop pails. Each received about a half pint of water daily. Some refused to eat. With their hearts fixed on death, these melancholy sufferers had no desire for sustenance. The ship's crew unceremoniously tossed the weak, the ill, and the dead overboard. The voyagers' survivors faced continued uncertainty and compulsory servitude an ocean away from their homes and families, after an unimaginably grueling voyage of anywhere between six weeks to three months.

Portugal's Prince Henry's lust for African gold forever altered the face of Africa and of the world. In 1442 Portuguese sailors returned home with gold dust and two handfuls of Africans, black gold. This initiated the Atlantic slave trade. Between the mid-1400s and the late 1800s European invaders transported between ten million and twelve million unwilling West Africans from their ancestral home, carrying them to Europe, the Americas, and the Caribbean Islands. Ghana, Sierra Leone, and Nigeria in West Africa lost many hunters, weavers, farmers, blacksmiths, sons, and daughters. The slave trade proved so profitable that the once-designated West African coast became known as the Slave Coast.

Human enslavement did not begin with fifteenth-century Europeans. Slavery has darkened human history for as long as humankind has traveled and conquered other lands and people. Joseph's envious brothers stripped him of his multicolored coat and sold him into slavery. Although Joseph rose from the status of slave to stand at the Pharaoh's side, a generation later a new Pharaoh came into power "who knew not Joseph" (Exodus 1:8), and Egyptians made slaves of the Israelites who had lived among them. Romans had Jewish and Christian slaves. Muslim traders shipped more African slaves to North Africa, the Middle East, and the coast of the Indian Ocean than Europeans transported across the Atlantic Ocean. Around the world, across the legions of time, victorious nations have routinely enslaved those they defeated; invading forces subdued and took hostage their enemies. African tribes themselves practiced slavery. African slavers provided slaves to the foreigners who paid the right price. What distinguishes the Atlantic slave trade from all others was the almost 300-year reign of hopelessness and the excessive indignities inflicted upon the enslaved. This style of racial, chattel slavery, with loss of all human rights, produced masses of pilgrims of sorrow with no hope for the morrow.

MIND MIXER: KWL CHART

1. Start a KWL chart on slavery.
2. In the first column, K, list everything you *know* about slavery. In the W column list what you *want* to know about slavery.
3. At the completion of this unit on the Atlantic slave trade, complete the L column with what you *learned*.

VOCABULARY

allegiance	endangered	patriot
artifact	enslavement	pilgrim
Atlantic slave trade	expatriate	sacred
bondage	heritage	servitude
captivity	hull	sustenance
chattel	indoctrinate	terrain
coalition	Judeo–Christian	transatlantic
communal	Muslim	unity
disenfranchisement	nautical	
domination	oppression	

FOLKLORE

Spirit of the Asante
(A Retelling of the Ashanti tale, "The Golden Stool")

▼▼▼▼▼

Long before great floating vessels arrived from across the waters with pale, bearded men, the Asante Kingdom stood divided. The Asante constantly fought among themselves. Some pledged allegiance to one chief; others wanted another. Because the Asante had no unity, their enemies easily defeated them. Nyankopon, ruler of the sky, angry and weary of his people feuding like little children, sent for Anotchi, the medicine man.

"The time has come for the Asante people to unify. Call the leaders together for a grand council. Tell them I, Nyankopon, will show them who has my blessing for king."

Straightaway, Anotchi gathered all the leaders of the Asante and gave them Nyankopon's message.

"Tell us, Anotchi, how long shall we look to the sky? What will the sign be?" the assembled chiefs demanded like spoiled children.

"Wait and watch," Anotchi advised. "Nyankopon will make his choice known presently."

As the chiefs anxiously looked to the sky, Nyankopon lowered a brilliant golden stool from the heavens and passed it over Chief Nana Osei Tutu three times.

"This stool of pure gold holds the spirit of the Asante," Anotchi announced to those gathered around. "Nyankopon has chosen Nana Osei Tutu as Asantehene, the king of all the Asante people."

Anotchi continued, "No one may sit on this stool. Protect it as a sign of Nyankopon's presence and of the unity of the Asante people. As long as the Asante honor the golden stool and follow the rightful king, the Asante will triumph over all their enemies."

So Nana Osei Tutu ruled the Asante wisely for many years, as did each chosen Asantehene after him. All invaders fell in defeat as long as the Asante guarded the golden stool. This ends the tale of the sacred stool.

▼▼▼▼▼

The Ashanti, or Asante, reigned as the most powerful kingdom in south-central Ghana until British domination at the onset of the 1900s. Osei Tutu united the divided Ashanti people in the late 1600s as the first ruler, or *Asantehene*. In West Africa each man had his own elaborately decorated wooden stool that he carried with him to assemblies to protect it from theft or from someone else sitting on it. The Ashanti believed their spirit resided in their personal stool. Upon a man's death, only his eldest son could sit on his stool. Like all legends, "The Golden Stool" has elements of fact. When the British defeated the Ashanti, they reportedly demanded to see the fabled golden stool. The golden stool remains secreted in the palace at Kumasi, the capital of the former Ashanti Kingdom (Knappert, 1986).

Reader Response Opportunity

Prewriting

1. Complete a Folklore Chart.
2. Make a timeline of the Asante/Ashanti Kingdom.

Open-Ended Response Opportunity

1. Does the Western or European world have anything comparable to the golden stool for rulers? Explain. Does any other culture have a legend or fairy tale similar to the legend of the golden stool? Explain.
2. What is the theme of this tale? Support your answer with details from the folktale.
3. The golden stool is a symbol of the Asante people. What objects, places, or monuments symbolize the American people? What best symbolizes you and your family? Explain.
4. What lessons can you and others learn from this tale?
5. Create another title for the tale and explain how your title relates to the tale.
6. Write a moral for the tale, or create a political cartoon that reflects its main idea.

TRADITIONAL SEA ISLAND FOOD FARE

Transported from the coast of West Africa to the Georgia and Carolina Sea Island, Gullah recipes favor fresh water fish and seafood. The menu at a Sea Island restaurant may have a choice of oyster stew, oyster dressing, boiled crabs, gumbo, and crab cakes. Recipes for sweet potato pie, yams, mustard greens, and collard greens, which are widely regarded as Southern fare, grace Carolina and Gullah cookbooks dating back to the latter half of the 1800s. Goobers (peanuts) and sesame-seed confections also have Gullah–West African connections (Beaufort, Gullah). These Sea Island foods, influenced by Creole, Southern, and West African cultures, reflect the unique Gullah heritage.

Reader Response Opportunity

1. Research Gullah/Sea Island foods. Make a collage or web showing these foods. Suggested Web sites:

    http://www.beaufort.sc.us/bftlib/gullah.ht (Search: Beaufort County Library).

    http://www.knowitall.org/gullahtales/gullah/traditions.html. (Search words: *Gullah recipes* or *Sea Island recipes*).

2. How have the geography and culture influenced the food fare of the Sea Islands?

3. Write a paragraph explaining how to eat crab legs.

4. Write an explanatory composition telling how to prepare a Sea Island specialty.

PICTURE BOOK SELECTIONS

Ibo Landing Legend

Among the Gullah people on the Georgia and South Carolina Sea Islands, a haunting legend endures of proud Ibo natives who either truly believed they could walk beneath the sea or who knowingly chose a watery death rather than slavery far from home.

In the Time of Drums.
Kim Siegelson. Illustrated by Brian Pinkney.
New York: Hyperion Books for Children, 1999.

Coretta Scott King Award.

In the Time of Drums presents one version of this legend, with a rejuvenated Grandmother Twi as the drum major and her grandson Mentu left behind to tell the story. Resounding rhythms echo across history and throughout the story. (*Objet trouve*: a cowry, a seashell)

Reader Response Opportunity

Graphic Organizer/Prewriting Strategy

1. Make a cluster or web showing the characteristics of Grandmother Twi.

2. List the sensory images used in the story.

Open-Ended Response Opportunity

1. If you were taken away from your home, what would you miss most? Explain.

2. Grandmother Twi teaches Mentu to work hard, play the drums, and be "strong-strong." Which character in *In the Time of Drums* demonstrates the greatest strength?

3. Do the Ibo people show strength or weakness by walking into the sea? Explain.

The Ebony Sea.
Irene Smalls. Illustrated by Jononye Lockard.
Stamford, CT: Longmeadow Press, 1995.

The Ebony Sea provides an alternate version of the legendary, proud Ibo captives who choose dignity beneath the sea rather than slavery in a distant land. In this version of the Ibo Landing legend, an unnamed woman silently leads her fellow travelers into the sea. (*Objet trouve:* a fragment of red fabric)

Reader Response Opportunity

Graphic Organizer

Make a Venn diagram or T-chart showing the similarities and differences between *Ebony Sea* and *In the Time of the Drums.*

Open-Ended Response Opportunity

1. What makes the people follow the woman with the red scarf?
2. Which is more important to the men and women who get off the ship, being free or being alive? How can you tell?
3. What do the captured Ibo men and women cherish more, life or freedom? Support your answer with evidence from the story.
4. Which book, *The Ebony Sea* or *In the Time of the Drums,* do you prefer? Why?
5. Which version of the Ibo Landing legend, *The Ebony Sea* or *In the Time of the Drums,* presents the clearest picture of the woman who leads the people back into the sea? Support your view with evidence from both accounts.
6. Which do you think you would have done: submitted to slavery and unknown horrors in a strange land or marched into the sea to certain death? Explain.
7. Which captives do you think showed more courage: those who lived in slavery or those who jumped ship or marched into the ocean to their death to avoid slavery? Why? Support your opinion with specific details.

Amistad Rising: A Story of Freedom.
Veronica Chambers. Illustrated by Paul Lee.
San Diego, CA: Harcourt Brace, 1998.

Based on real events, *Amistad Rising* retells the story of Joseph Cinque and his countrymen and their historic legal victory. After taking control of the slave ship that holds him hostage, Cinque and his shipmates stand trial for mutiny. An impressive, historic courtroom victory allows Joseph Cinque to return to his West African home and family. (*Objet trouve*: miniature ship, chain link, miniature gavel, or scale of justice)

Reader Response Opportunity

Graphic Organizer

Make a Cycle Graph or Ring Graph showing the events surrounding the *Amistad.*

Open-Ended Response Opportunity

1. (Grades 3–5) The word *amistad* means friendship in Spanish. What examples of friendship are shown in the happenings surrounding the slave ship *Amistad?*

2. Is Joseph Cinque a good leader to the other men on the ship? Why?

3. In your opinion, when does Joseph Cinque show more courage: when he attacks the crew of the *Amistad* or when he fights in the courts of the United States? Explain.

4. What actions in *Amistad Rising* demonstrate Joseph Cinque's leadership, intelligence, and determination in his fight for his freedom?

5. Explain the irony of the name *Amistad* for the slave ship. What other examples of irony can you think of in American history or current events?

NOVEL SELECTIONS

Amos Fortune: Free Man.
Elizabeth Yates. Illustrated by Nora Unwin.
New York: Puffin Books, 1950.

Newbery Medal.

The intense, solemn beating of drums foreshadows impending tragedy in the opening of *Amos Fortune: Free Man*. At-mun, son of a king, gently dances with his sister at a village gathering. Then slavers, black and white, crash the party and take At-mun and other villagers captives. Forty-five years later At-mun, renamed Amos, reclaims his freedom in the land that held him captive.

Reader Response Opportunity

Graphic Organizer

Make a timeline or Bio Graph of Amos Fortune's life.

Open-Ended Response Opportunity

1. Is Violet wrong to bury Amos's kettle of coins? Why?

2. "The years between have shown me that it does a man no good to be free until he learns how to live, how to walk in step with God," asserts Amos Fortune (Yates, 162). In your opinion, does Amos Fortune learn how to live? Does he walk in step with God? Explain your answers.

Praisesong for the Widow.
Paule Marshall.
New York: Penguin, 1983.

While on a West Indies cruise, unsettling dreams and feelings propel Avey Johnson, widow, out of her comfortable lifestyle and into a cultural journey of the soul. Avey accompanies a peculiar old man on an excursion to an island and through experiences that awaken within her memories of childhood visits to her Great-aunt Cuney's Sea Island on the South Carolina Tidewater: the Ring Shout, the Landing, and Ibos stepping resolutely into the sea.

Reader Response Opportunity

1. How does Avey's great-aunt's account of the Ibo Landing affair compare to the ones in *Ebony Sea* and *In the Time of Drums*?

2. Why do you believe this legend has lasted all these years?

3. Avey's traveling companion, Thomasina Moore, accuses Avey of being crazy and selfish for leaving the cruise unexpectedly. What do you think happens to Avey?

4. How does Avey change after leaving the cruise and meeting Lebert Joseph?

5. Keep a log of your reflections as you read *Praisesong for the Widow*.

6. What does *Praisesong for the Widow* say to you about life, heritage, history, family, and memories?

7. What one word or sentence would you use to describe this book? Explain.

NONFICTION SELECTIONS

Spirit Dive: An African-American's Journey to Uncover a Sunken Slave Ship's Past.
Michael Cottman.
New York: Crown Publishers, 2000.

Scuba diver and journalist Cottman retraces the history of the slave ship *Henrietta Marie,* which sank off the Florida coast in 1700. As a member of an interracial, international crew of deep-sea divers, Cottman examined the wreckage of the *Henrietta Marie. Spirit Dive* carries the reader on a doomed trip during a shameful time in the history of the world.

Read aloud the first three pages and selected segments of Chapters 1 through 4. Especially read the bottom of page 28 about the discovery of the shackles among the 7,000 artifacts and call students' attention to the photographs in Chapter 13. Then challenge students to check out the book from the library and to continue reading it on their own.

Reader Response Opportunity

Prewriting

Have students record their thoughts daily in a reflection log as they listen to excerpts from *Spirit Dive* and as they view the photographs in the book.

Open-Ended Response Opportunity

1. Beginning in 1983 divers discovered numerous artifacts from the site of the wreckage of the *Henrietta Marie.* Which discovery do you believe is most memorable to the author of *Spirit Dive*? Explain your answer.

2. In Chapter 4 the author expresses his rage against Tournay, the merchant who made iron shackles for slaves. Yet, during Tournay's lifetime, poor London children and Tournay's servants regarded him as generous. In your opinion, does Tournay qualify as a saint or a sinner? Why?

3. Why do you think Tournay's actions toward his servants and the poor in London contradicted his involvement with the slave trade?

4. In what other incidents in the book might different people see different sides of a person's personality? Explain.

5. What lessons does Michael Cottman glean from his journey into the past of the *Henrietta Marie*? What lessons can you learn from Cottman's experiences?

MULTIMEDIA

The Gullah Culture.
Bradford Pazant.
http://www.ncat.edu/~pazantb/.

On this site the reader will find detailed background facts about the Sea Islands and the origin of the Gullah culture. The photographs on the site allow viewers to see the islands.

The Moonlit Road—Ibo Landing.
http://www.mr.com/ibo/ibo_cbg002.html.

At this site students can read about the Nigerian home of the Ibos. The site details parallels between the terrain of the Niger Delta marshlands from which the Ibos came and the muddy marshes of the Sea Islands. Also, students can read a moving variation of the Ibo Landing legend. The black background makes a haunting canvas for this portrait of courage.

Reader Response Opportunity

Graphic Organizer

Make a Venn diagram showing the similarities and differences between either *The Ebony Sea* or *In the Time of Drums* and the Oba version of the Ibo Landing legend.

Open-Ended Response Opportunity

Write a composition comparing and contrasting two versions of the Ibo Landing legend.

I Am Sapelo.
Cornelia Bailey.
http://www.gacoast.com/navigator/iamsapelo.html.

Gullah Sea Island storyteller Cornelia Walker Bailey presents her endangered island and culture in a stream of remembrances and with the ease of a relative sitting on the front porch passing the time of day.

Reader Response Opportunity

Graphic Organizer

Make a T-chart listing the pros and cons of staying on the island.

Open-Ended Response Opportunity

1. Write an autobiographical narrative of any poignant childhood memories you have.

2. Progress threatens the future of centuries-old traditions on Sapelo Island. In your opinion, which is more important to protect: the past and its traditions or the future and its progress? Explain.

Research Topics

Research one of the following topics and narrow it down to a specific area, such as the effect of progress on the Gullah culture on Sapelo Island. Write a research paper, create a visual representation, or make a PowerPoint presentation.

Igbo, or Ibo, people

Ibo Landing legend

Sapelo Island

St. Simon's Island

Gullah culture

Geechee culture

Carolina or Georgia Sea Islands

Niger Delta marshland

Amistad Mystic Seaport.
http://amistad.mysticseaport.org/timeline/amistad.html or
http://amistad.mysticseaport.org/library/news/nyca/1839.09.05.fundsappeal.html
        (Search word: *Amistad*).

These sites offer maps, timelines, newspaper articles, biographies, sketches, diary and journal entries, trial transcripts, and nautical charts relevant to the *Amistad* incident.

Reader Response Opportunity

1. Why do you think the Supreme Court decided to give Joseph Cinque and the rest of the *Amistad* passengers their freedom?

2. Should the *Amistad* uprising by the West Africans be considered mutiny or self-defense? Why?

The Voyage of La Amistad: A Quest for Freedom (Video).
MPI Home Video, 1997.

This 70-minute educational documentary video of the *Amistad* narrated by Alfre Woodard suits the classroom better than Steven Spielberg's R-rated *Amistad* (1998).

Reader Response Opportunity

Prewriting Strategy: Reflection Log

Have students write their reflections on the video for 5 to 7 minutes.

Open-Ended Response Opportunity: Secondary

During the *Amistad* proceedings, President John Quincy Adams declared that humankind's natural state is freedom and that people will do anything to regain it. What in the *Amistad* events supports this?

The Middle Passage: White Ships/Black Cargo.
Author and photographer, Tom Feelings.
http://www.juneteenth.com/index.html.
New York: Dial Books for Young Readers, 1995.

The photographs of Tom Feelings sear the emotions as the misery of the Middle Passage swells from the images.

Reader Response Opportunity

1. Have students record their personal reactions to the images.
2. Have students select one image and write about it.

The Middle Passage Foundation, Inc.
http://www.tmpf.org/history.htm.

This site contains a brief exposition of the history of the Middle Passage and a timeline.

Reader Response Opportunity

1. Ask students to select one event on the timeline and discuss its significance on slavery and on the history of the United States.
2. Have students discuss their selected event's impact on life in the twenty-first century.

Africans in America.
http://www.pbs.org/wgbh/aia/home.html.

This PBS site has text, visuals, a teacher's guide, a youth activity guide, information on an educational television series and video, and a resource bank of visuals and text covering the Atlantic Slave trade from its onset to Africans in America from the end of the Civil War.

Reader Response Opportunity

1. Research slavery throughout history. Write your conclusion about humankind and slavery.
2. Compare and contrast the oppression and liberation of African American slaves to the Hebrew bondage in Egypt.

WRITING PROMPTS

Elementary Writing Prompt 1

The Ibo people believed the water would carry them back to their West African homeland. They felt a connection to their country in the Niger Delta marshland and risked their lives to get back home.

> Write about the importance of the country you call home.

Elementary Writing Prompt 2

Joseph Cinque showed courage by fighting in court for his freedom.

> Write about someone showing great courage.

Secondary Writing Prompt 1

Joseph Cinque and his fellow travelers overcame seemingly insurmountable obstacles to regain their liberty, and they displayed great endurance and determination.

> Write about obtaining victory through endurance and determination.

Secondary Writing Prompt 2

The Gullah people who live on the Georgia and Carolina Sea Islands follow many traditions brought over from Africa by their ancestors.

> Write about the importance of cultural traditions.

Multilevel Writing Prompt

The *Henrietta Marie* personifies horrific greed and barbaric treatment.

> Identify a symbol of evil.
> Explain how this symbol characterizes evil.

5
▼▼▼▼▼

Get on Board: The Underground Railroad

When spider webs unite, they can tie up a lion.
——Ethiopian proverb

Get on Board, Little Children

Get on board, little children.
Get on board, little children.
Get on board, little children.
There's room for many a more.

The gospel train's a coming,
I hear it just at hand.
I hear the train wheels moving,
And rumbling through the land.

Get on board, little children.
Get on board, little children.
Get on board, little children.
There's room for many a more.

HISTORICAL CONTEXT

From the inception of the Atlantic slave trade, innumerable enslaved Africans in America attempted to board the freedom train. Mutiny, rebellions, pleas for liberty, and escapes served as boarding passes. Music with hidden messages called out the "All aboard" for passengers on the Underground Railway. Slave owners, fearful of drums' communication potential, banned drums among African slaves after unsuccessful rebellions, but they allowed the singing of spirited religious songs because they believed the songs pacified the slaves and made them submissive. Resolute, courageous Underground Railway conductors and agents devised crafty methods, using slave songs or quilts with hidden messages to inform and alert furtive freedom seekers. Fueled by hope, desperation, and an insatiable hunger for liberty, more than 100,000 men, women, and children shed the bonds of slavery and headed for the northern states and Canada by means of the Freedom Train.

Quakers, free Blacks, abolitionists, ex-slaves, males, and females acted as agents and conductors on the Underground Railroad. Harriet Tubman ranks as the preeminent Underground Railroad conductor, risking her liberty and life time after time to lead others to free territories. Other active, well-known advocates for the abolition of slavery include Josiah Henson, Susan B. Anthony, Lucretia Mott, and Frederick Douglass. This complex, covert network smuggled a nominal number of men, women, and children into free territory. "Get on board, little children. Get on board."

MIND MIXER: LISTING

1. Have students, in groups of 3 to 4, discuss everything they know about the Underground Railroad.
2. A group secretary can write down the group's Responses Opportunity, or a group representative can read aloud the answers as the teacher or a scribe lists them on the board or on butcher paper.

VOCABULARY

abolition	complacent	Good Samaritan	legendary	origin	refugee
abolitionist	concoction	gourd	liberty	parched	safehouse
advocate	conductor	Holocaust	lineage	plumage	submissive
agriculture	covert	human rights	maize	poultry	sustenance
aroma	endorse	immigrant	millet	preamble	sympathizer
benevolent	fowl	inalienable rights	mutiny	preeminent	tantalizing
bondservant	freedman	indentured	network	prohibitions	union
collaboration	fugitive	injustice	neutral	rebellion	violations

FOLKLORE

The African Mourning Dove and the Royal Guinea Fowl
(Adapted from an Ashanti freedom fable)

▼▼▼▼▼

Once and long ago two friends, the African Mourning Dove and the Royal Guinea Fowl, lived in a country now known as Kenya in the eastern region of the rich, African continent. Mourning Dove and Guinea Fowl frequently visited with one another but chose to take separate paths to seek their daily sustenance. African Mourning Dove found fulfillment in flying over the grasslands, scrubs, and thorn bushes and looking for tasty insects, nuts, seeds, and fruit as night yielded to a new day. Royal Guinea Fowl, on the other hand, preferred not to hunt for food; she instead looked to be fed from the hand of a benevolent villager.

As was her custom, one day Royal Guinea Fowl set off for a nearby Kikuyu village and roosted atop a tall coconut palm tree hoping some generous Kikuyu woman might notice her stately beauty and feel disposed to share a few beans or seeds and give her fresh well water to soothe her parched throat. By chance, just as Guinea Fowl had hoped, a farmer's wife gladly tied Guinea Fowl to the coconut tree and fed the hen handfuls of maize kernels. Early the next morning the farmer's wife brought Guinea Fowl more grains of millet than she could eat and filled her dish with cool water.

One early morning, three days later, as Dove flew over the village en route to the grasslands, she spotted her friend, Guinea Fowl. "Hen, who has put a rope around your neck and bound you to that tree? Shall I help you get free?"

"Free?" Guinea Fowl asked laughingly, strutting around the coconut tree like a cocky pheasant. "Why would I want to be free? This peasant woman appreciates my striking good looks and my beautiful plumage. She rises early to feed me! I never go hungry. Food fit for a queen: rice, maize, peas, the greenest leaves. This woman and her family know how to treat royalty! Meanwhile you wake early and wear yourself out each day searching for seeds, insects, nuts, or fruit. No larva for me. No more scratching and pecking for me," the foolish fowl bragged.

"Well," huffed Dove, "I'd rather be free and hungry than have a rope around my neck." This said, Dove left to gather her food for the day.

Under the shade of the coconut palm tree, Royal Guinea Hen grew lazy, plump, and complacent. A fortnight later as Mourning Dove once more passed over Guinea Fowl's new home, she noticed her friend no longer sat tied to the coconut tree. Instead, an old goat lay tethered to the tree. "Good morning, Baba Goat. Can you tell me where my friend Guinea Fowl is?"

"Your friend, the guinea fowl? Oh, I am sorry to tell you this. I believe the farmer's wife fattened her up and prepared a delicious stew for her family. Ah, yes! The tantalizing aroma of mint, yams, onions, and fowl simmering with the perfect blend of spices drew me to this humble dwelling. Now the farmer's kindly wife feeds me to my heart's content. Why, I have gained five pounds since I arrived! I wonder what luscious concoction she will cook up next."

"Coo, coo," Dove sang mournfully as she flew away, reflecting on happier times with her noble friend.

It is better to scratch for a living and be free than to be fed by a stranger's hand and end up in the cooking pot.

▼▼▼▼▼

This freedom fable has its origins among the Ashanti people of the Gold Coast, perhaps in what is now Ghana, with a dove and a hen as the main characters. In this version, the story moves to Kenya, home to Streptopelia Decipiens, the African Mourning Dove, and Acryllium Vulturinum, the Vulturine Guinea Fowl, a colorful cousin to the pheasant. The Guinea Fowl or Guinea Hen seeks a handout among the Kikuyu, traditionally sheep and goat farmers and the largest ethnic group of Kenya. Baba (Father) Goat most likely faces an end similar to the Guinea Fowl. Recipes for goat meat abound, and goatskin also makes superb drums.

Reader Response Opportunity

1. Create a comic strip that shows the main events of the story or complete a Folklore Chart.

2. What lessons for living can the reader learn from this freedom fable?

3. What do you think will happen to Baba Goat (Primary/Elementary)? What examples of foreshadowing can be found in this tale (Secondary/Post-Secondary)?

4. Why do people sometimes willingly sacrifice their freedoms?

5. Only a small percentage of enslaved African Americans chose to get on board the Underground Railroad. Most remained in bondage and longed for freedom. Which path would you choose? Do you think you would go underground to escape or would you continue to labor as a slave? Explain.

TRADITIONAL ASHANTI FOWL FOOD FARE

Kuku (chicken, guinea hen, or guinea fowl) frequently functions as the main ingredient in West African recipes. Chefs and historians debate the origin of Ashanti Chicken, deboned chicken stuffed with yams and more chicken (*Congo Cookbook*). What Ghanaian cook, a Fanti or an Ashanti, first pictured stuffing a chicken with more chicken and sweet yams, mint, onions, and tomatoes? Chicken à la Ashantee, or Ashanti Chicken, stands out in the memories of those travelers blessed to experience tasting it in the nineteenth century. Richard Francis Burton and Robert Hamil Nassau, nineteenth-century travelers to West Africa, both described this classic, rich Gold Coast poultry creation in their writings (*Congo Cookbook*).

Reader Response Opportunity

1. Research the Guinea fowl. Make a Venn diagram or T-chart showing the similarities between chicken and guinea fowl. Suggested site:

   http://www.congocookbook.com.

   (Search: *Congo Cookbook*).

2. How do traditional sub-Saharan African methods of cooking chicken differ from popular American chicken dishes? In what ways do the African methods reflect the sub-Saharan African culture, agriculture, and geography?

3. Find an African poultry recipe. Write a composition explaining how to prepare the entrée.

PICTURE BOOK SELECTIONS

Barefoot: Escape on the Underground Railroad.
Pamela Duncan. Illustrated by Henry Cole.
New York: HarperCollins, 1997.

As the nameless, faceless barefoot man flees trackers who want to take him back to slavery, the elements of nature covertly come to his assistance. *Barefoot* makes an excellent companion to *Follow the Drinking Gourd* (1988) by Jeanette Winter. (*Objet trouve:* traced footprint)

Reader Response Opportunity

Prewriting Strategy

Make a web showing everything that helps the Barefoot escape the Heavy Boots.

Open-Ended Response Opportunity

1. Do the animals and plants want Barefoot to escape the slave trackers? How can you tell? Give specific evidence from the story.
2. What other ways can nature help us when we are lost or afraid?
3. Do you think the animals know they are helping Barefoot? Explain.
4. How does the use of figurative language and sensory images make the story come alive?
5. Why does the author not give Barefoot a name or face? What effect does this have?

Follow the Drinking Gourd.
Written and illustrated by Jeanette Winter.
New York: Dragonfly Books, 1988.

Legendary sailor and sympathizer Peg Leg Joe hires himself out as a handyman to masters of Southern plantations. As Peg Leg Joe treks from plantation to plantation, he teaches the plantations' slaves the folk song, "Follow the Drinking Gourd," with freedom's secrets cloaked in each line. A family threatened by impending separation answers the quail's call and follows the drinking gourd to safety. (*Objet trouve:* gourd seed)

Reader Response Opportunity

1. How do you think Molly, James, Old Hattie, little Isaiah, and George feel as they flee from men and dogs in the blanket of darkness?
2. How does the family of five survive while on the run? Do you believe you could have survived like this? Explain.
3. Author Jeanette Winter refers to the family of runaways by their names. Does the use of individual names make the reader more or less sympathetic to the characters? Explain.

Aunt Harriet's Underground Railroad in the Sky.
Faith Ringgold. Illustrated by J. Davis.
Boston: Horn Book, 1992.

Jane Addams Picture Book Award, 1993.

Faith Ringgold puts a magical, fairy tale spin on the excursions of Harriet Tubman. The illustrations coupled with Ringgold's lively language breathe life into the already amazing accomplishments of the Black Moses who spirited many of her own into the arms of freedom. Ms. Ringgold's Fantasia-like, mystical approach to history and African American oral tradition sets her apart from other writers. Young readers addicted to Harry Potter-type fantasy will enjoy Ringgold's adaptations.

Reader Response Opportunity

Prewriting Strategies

1. List some of the vivid descriptions found in the book.
2. List any examples of figurative language.

Graphic Organizer

Make a timeline of Harriet Tubman's life.

Intercultural Book Comparison/Graphic Organizer

1. Read *Abuela* (New York: Dutton, 1991) by Arthur Dorros or *In Rosa's Mexico* (New York: Alfred A. Knopt, 1996) by Campbell Geeslin. Both picture books celebrate Hispanic heritage and have protagonists who are young dreamers and who take flight. Discuss other similar books.
2. Make a Venn diagram comparing and contrasting any two of the books.

Sweet Clara and the Freedom Quilt.
Deborah Hopkinson. Illustrated by James Ransome.
New York: Dragonfly Books, 1993.

IRA Children's Book Award.

Using her limited knowledge of the land and the bits and pieces of information she hears from other people, Clara, a young girl, painstakingly quilts a map to freedom. The work of her hands—her map quilt—guides Clara and others to freedom's sanctuary. (*Objet trouve:* quilt scraps)

Reader Response Opportunity

Prewriting Strategy

1. Make a T-chart.
2. In the first column, list the scraps Clara uses in her quilt.
3. In the second column, list what each scrap represents.

Open-Ended Response Opportunity

1. Define symbolism. Explain the designs Clara employs to represent various places on the escape route. Will other slaves understand the symbols so that they can use the quilt map to get safely away after Clara is gone? Explain.
2. Clara manages to rescue her family and escape even though she does not take the quilt with her. Why do you think this is possible?
3. What other people in history have used secret signals and passages to thwart the enemy and preserve their liberty? Explain.
4. Why do songs make effective tools to communicate secret messages?
5. What might be other ways for messages/signals to be secretly passed along?
6. How are gangs and secret societies similar to the secret network of the Underground Railroad? Give specific details.

Multimedia Response Opportunity

1. Make a map using construction paper, the computer, or any other method to show the path from your school to a safe place.
2. Use symbols your classmates and other peers will recognize.

Under the Quilt of Night.
Deborah Hopkinson. Illustrated by James Ransome.
New York: Atheneum Books, 2001.

In *Under the Quilt of Night* a child retells the story of her escape with other slaves. Night's black quilt, wagons, and safehouses shield the runaways as they make their way north. (*Objet trouve:* black cloth)

Reader Response Opportunity

1. Prewriting: List the things in the book that represent safety.
2. Graphic Organizer: Make a Cycle Graph showing the events of the book.
3. Compare this book to one of the other Underground Railroad picture books.

NOVEL SELECTIONS

Which Way Freedom?
Joyce Hansen.
New York: Avon Books, 1986.

Coretta Scott King Honor Book; ALA Notable Book.

Obi, a slave in South Carolina, perseveres in his dreams of running away, seeing his mother, and finding freedom. En route to freedom he spends time with Rebel soldiers and with Union soldiers.

Reader Response Opportunity

Prewriting Strategy

Make a Bio Graph of Obi's life.

Open-Ended Response Opportunity

Buka tells Obi, "You got to learn which way freedom be. It here first. In you own mind" (Hansen, 1986).

1. In your opinion, does Buka find freedom?
2. Does Obi find freedom? Explain.
3. The Underground Railroad had secret stations that served as rest stops and safehouses for runaway slaves. What types of safehouses does modern society have? Explain.

The House of Dies Drear.
Virginia Hamilton. Illustrated by Eros Keith.
New York: Simon & Schuster, Inc. 1968.

Edgar Alan Poe Award; *School Library Journal* Best Book.

Thomas Small learns about himself, the Drear house, his heritage, and the Underground Railway when he moves to a new home in Ohio. The house of abolitionist Dies Drear holds many secrets, and the first half of the Drear House miniseries offers suspense and history.

Reader Response Opportunity

Open-Ended Response Opportunity

1. How does his family's move affect Thomas Small?
2. In your opinion, which is the most valuable secret or treasure Thomas uncovers? Explain.

Research

1. Research the Underground Railroad in Ohio.
2. Research secret passageways/tunnels in history (Examples: the Roman Empire and Christians, World War II and the Jews, postwar East Berlin and the Berlin Wall).
3. Compare these to hidden tunnels and passageways used during the enslavement of African Americans.

NONFICTION SELECTIONS

Many Thousand Gone: African Americans from Slavery to Freedom.
Virginia Hamilton. Illustrated by Leo and Diane Dillon.
New York: Alfred A. Knopf, 1993.

1994 ALA Notable Children's Books.

Virginia Hamilton drew her title from a recurrent phrase in the following sorrowful slave song, "No more auction block for me, no more, no more. No more auction block for me, many thousand gone." *Many Thousand Gone* complements Hamilton's *The People Could Fly* and gives powerful testimony to the courage and perseverance of enslaved Africans in America.

Reader Response Opportunity

Individual Response Opportunity

1. Explain the title.
2. Summarize your favorite selection.
3. Explain why it is your favorite.
4. What does it tell you about the time period in American history?
5. What does it tell you about life for some African Americans during that period?

Book Talk

1. Get into a small group (2–4) of people who selected the same selection.
2. Discuss your response.
3. Get into a group of people who selected different stories.
4. Talk about your selection.

Hidden in Plain View: A Secret Story of Quilts and the Underground Railroad.
Jacqueline L. Tobin.
New York: Doubleday, 1999.

Hidden in Plain View unravels the secret code of the Underground Railroad as it appeared on quilts. The artistry and ingenuity inherent in the quilt designs pay homage to the African heritage of the quilt makers. The text includes black-and-white and color prints of quilt patterns and quilts. Call students' attention to the photographs in Chapter 13.

Reader Response Opportunity

Open-Ended Response Opportunity

The foreword in *Hidden in Plain View* says, "Arts preserve cultural traditions."

1. How do we see this in *Hidden in Plain View*?
2. Describe other examples of art preserving the traditions of a culture.
3. Quilts are called "fabric authors" because they tell stories and keep history. What other forms of "authors" do we have in today's society? Explain.
4. Do comedians, preachers, and teachers qualify as authors? Explain your answer.
5. Historians often do not assign much credibility to oral tradition. How important and valid do you believe oral tradition is?

MULTIMEDIA

The Underground Railroad.
http://www.nationalgeographic.com/features/99/railroad/.
(Search words: *Underground Railroad*).

This Web site includes a timeline, pictures, and biographies of prominent abolitionists and Underground Railroad agents.

Reader Response Opportunity

1. Write a week of diary entries from the point of view of a runaway or a person who assists runaways at a safehouse.

2. Pretend you are a journalist and write an interview between yourself and someone involved with the Underground Railroad. First, write at least five questions. Then, based on what you have learned about the person and the Underground Railroad, write the person's answers.

3. An elaborate network of Quakers, abolitionists, escaped slaves, freedmen, and other anti-slavery sympathizers assisted runaways in their escape to freedom. Why did strangers risk their own lives and freedom to help the fugitives?

Underground Railroad (Video).
A&E Entertainment, 1999.

This History Channel 100-minute video narrated by Alfre Woodard tells the story of the network that led to the successful escape of more than 100,000 slaves. It serves as a perfect preamble or closure to a study of the Underground Railroad.

Reader Response Opportunity

Underground Railroad agents and conductors collaborated to help Africans enslaved in the American South escape to the North or to Canada despite laws that endorsed slavery and protected slave owners. In the twentieth and twenty-first centuries, American citizens smuggle illegal immigrants from Mexico and Central America into the United States. Additionally, our government sometimes facilitates the defection to the United States of citizens from countries suspected of human rights violations.

1. How are these practices similar to and different from assisting escaped slaves?

2. How does the Underground Railroad compare to hiding and helping Jews and other targets of the Nazis during the Holocaust?

WRITING PROMPTS

Elementary Writing Prompt

The passengers on the Underground Railroad faced dangers as they escaped and severe consequences if they were recaptured. However, the secret network of agents, conductors, and safe-houses cooperated to make numerous escapes possible.

> Write about using cooperation to accomplish something good.

Secondary Writing Prompt

The Underground Railroad proved successful in carrying unknown numbers of slaves to freedom. Those involved in the secret network planned very carefully to ensure their own safety and the safety of the passengers.

> Write about planning for success.

Multilevel Writing Prompt

Many men, women, and children made the decision to find freedom and a better life through the Underground Railroad.

> Write about making a life-changing decision.

6
▼▼▼▼▼

Let My People Go:
Emancipation's Plea

A loose tooth will not rest until it is pulled out.

—Ethiopian proverb

Go Down, Moses

When Israel was in Egypt land, let my people go.
Oppressed so hard they could not stand, let my people go.

Go down, Moses, way down in Egypt land.
Tell ole Pharaoh, let my people go.

Thus saith the Lord, bold Moses said, let my people go.
If not I'll smite thy first-born dead. Let my people go.

No more shall they in bondage toil. Let my people go.
Let them come out with Egypt's spoil. Let my people go.

Go down, Moses, way down in Egypt land.
Tell ole Pharaoh, let my people go.

HISTORICAL CONTEXT

"Give us free." "Loosen my shackles." "Set me free." "Let my people go." Petitions for emancipation cried out from bowed down heads, pleading eyes, and burdened hearts. Men and women, enslaved for the color of their skin, hungered for the taste of freedom. African Americans challenged the institution of slavery by seeking justice in the courts of their abductors or by petitioning their owners or other men in high places. Many who had the opportunity to earn money toiled and saved enough money to purchase their own freedom and that of their loved ones. Others trapped in slavery's rocky place wrestled with God's angel, waiting for the break of day.

Freedmen, enslaved African Americans, and ex-slaves actively worked for the eradication of slavery. Frederick Douglass, an ex-slave and respected abolitionist, crusaded for the elimination of slavery in his journalistic writings and impassioned speeches. Bannaky, the grandfather of Benjamin Banneker, had his freedom granted to him by the woman who bought him, grew to love him as a friend, and chose him as her husband. Bannaky's grandson, eighteenth-century scientist and inventor Benjamin Banneker, dispatched his appeal to President Thomas Jefferson in a missive reminiscent of the Declaration of Independence.

York, the enslaved Black man who accompanied Lewis and Clark on their famed expedition seeking a water passageway to the Pacific Ocean, repeatedly asked Captain William Clark for his freedom. A more benevolent yet equally reluctant pharaoh, Captain Clark persisted in his refusal to set York free. African Americans aligned with Union troops, hoping to help them defeat the slave states and win their liberty. Each carried the same message: Let my people go.

MIND MIXER: PERSUASION

1. Have students think of one issue important enough for them to appeal to someone to change it. Give them time to think about it and prepare to defend it. What is the issue? Whom would they ask? Why?

2. Divide students into small groups of 2 to 4.

3. Set a timer for 7 to 10 minutes and let students discuss their issue and attempt to persuade their groupmates to agree with them.

4. When the timer rings, solicit volunteers to talk about a classmate who successfully persuaded them.

VOCABULARY

armory	hostility	maroon	replica
arsenal	hypocritical	missive	resistance
barbarous	hypocrisy	mulatto	revolutionary
casualties	informant	Old Testament	sabotage
conspiracy	institution	petition	segregated
descent	insurrection	pygmy	suppress
emancipation	integrated	quell	tyranny
eradication	manual labor	regimen	vagabond
expedition			

FOLKLORE

A Lion, a Goat, and a Hunter
(A retelling of "The Lion and the Goat")

▼▼▼▼▼

In the land and time of my ancestors, a pygmy goat leisurely grazed on the fertile grasslands in the cool of the morning. The tiny goat wandered from one lush clump of tall grass to the next, remembering to cast her eyes about for fallen banana leaves to add variety to her meal. Pygmy Goat rambled and nibbled, scarcely chewing the nourishing grass and leaves before moving to the next cluster of vegetation. Her peaceful reverie was broken by a dreadful wail.

"I'm doomed! I'm doomed! How foolishly I have behaved! If only I had not been starving, this would never have happened."

Pygmy Goat tracked the woeful sounds until she spotted the object of her search. A lion, thorny paws cradling his royal head, sat trapped in a hunter's snare. Exhausted and thin, the lion rocked on his bony haunches with rivers of tears in his large eyes. Pygmy Goat, fearful but curious, drew closer to the ensnared enemy.

"Dear fellow, whatever are you doing in there causing such a ruckus this fine morning?"

The lion had so busied himself in self-pity that he had not even noticed the pygmy goat's cautious approach.

"Oh, Insignificant One! You startled me sneaking up on me in my moment of misery. I suppose you rejoice in seeing me in this condition, waiting without hope until the pitiless hunter returns for his prey. Well, now that you have seen me, leave. Have the decency to allow me some privacy in my affliction."

"Rejoice? Why, not at all!" protested Pygmy Goat. "I must admit your type and mine do not share the same tastes in food, but it saddens me to see you trapped in this manner. After all, we have the same two-legged enemy. Why, I would help if I could! But you are a lion after all, and I am a mere goat. You do look famished. How do I know I would not be your next meal?"

"My next meal! If I get out of this trap, my teeth will never again bite into goat flesh," assured Lion. "My taste for goat meat got me in trouble in the first place. As you can surely see, the meat supply has gotten low. The hunters' snares catch more than we poor lions do. You can imagine how relieved I was yesterday evening when I smelled and then caught sight of a hindquarter of goat meat. Alas, as soon as I closed my jaws over the meat, this cage dropped over me. No more goat meat for me. I always did prefer antelope."

Being a naturally tenderhearted and helpful creature, Pygmy Goat set about bucking her horns against Lion's cage. After much effort by the small animal, and with no assistance but much unsolicited advice from the lion, the trap sprang open. Immediately Lion seized Pygmy Goat, planning to devour his rescuer. As Pygmy Goat struggled and pleaded with Lion to honor his promise, the hunter appeared to check his trap.

"What do I have here? I seemed to have trapped both a goat and a lion. My family shall have milk, wool, and meat. What good luck!"

Pygmy Goat recalled too late a wise saying from the elders:

Nothing is more dangerous than saving a hungry beast.

▼▼▼▼▼

Reader Response Opportunity

1. What figurative language does the tale use? Explain.
2. What might have happened if the lion had kept his promise to the pygmy goat? Explain.
3. What lessons can you learn from the lion's actions and the pygmy goat's actions?
4. What are the consequences and benefits of helping someone in danger?
5. What things in life do people allow to trap them? Explain.
6. How does this tale relate to the attempts to emancipate America's slaves?

TRADITIONAL GOAT FOOD FARE

Goats abound in Africa: the African pygmy goat featured in "A Lion, a Goat, and a Hunter," the Nigerian blue-eyed dwarf, the Nigerian Dwarf, the Nubian goat, the West African dwarf, the Sahel, and the Red Sokoto. West Africans raise Red Sokoto and pygmy goats for their meat. Goat pepper soup, goat stew, egusi soup, okra soup, ogbono soup, biriani, oluwambo, smoked goat meat, brochettes, bushmeat, goat's milk, and goat steak—goat makes an appearance in numerous sub-Saharan African dishes.

Reader Response Opportunity

1. Research Nigerian goat dishes, and name and describe one.
2. Research sub-Saharan goat dishes. Name and describe a sub-Saharan dish with goat meat.
3. Because of its difficulty with agriculture, Africa today typically places less emphasis on raising animals for meat. How might that affect traditional African recipes?
4. Write an explanatory composition telling how to prepare a dish with goat meat.

PICTURE BOOK SELECTIONS

Molly Bannaky.
Alice McGill. Illustrated by Chris Soenpiet.
Boston: Houghton Mifflin, 1999.

Molly Walsh, an English bondservant, comes to the colonies for seven years of indentured service after spilling her master's pail of milk. Molly buys a slave. Eventually Molly and Bannaky fall in love. Molly frees and marries him, defying prohibitions against such marriages. Bannaky and Molly become the grandparents of Benjamin Banneker. (*Objet trouve:* anything with a cow/dairy motif)

Reader Response Opportunity

Graphic Organizer

Draw Molly's family tree.

Open-Ended Response Opportunity

1. Is Molly's punishment for spilling her master's milk fair? Why?

2. English law forces Molly Walsh to come to this country for seven years of service as an indentured servant. Is an indentured servant better off than a slave? How? (Grades 6–12)

3. Molly, a former bondservant, buys a slave to help her clear land, but she plans to free him later. In your opinion, was there ever a good reason to own a slave? Explain.

Dear Benjamin Banneker.
Andrea Davis. Illustrated by Brian Pinkney.
San Diego, CA: Voyager Books, 1994.

Benjamin Banneker—astronomer, mathematician, maker of the first clock in the American colonies, and the first African American to receive a presidential appointment—writes a letter to President Thomas Jefferson protesting Jefferson's ownership of slaves. (*Objet trouve:* miniature clock/watch, star)

Reader Response Opportunity

Prewriting Strategy

List all of Benjamin Banneker accomplishments and inventions.

Open-Ended Response Opportunity

1. Choose one of Banneker's inventions or accomplishments and explain how your life might be different without it.

2. Unlike many early African Americans, Benjamin Banneker attended school with other children in a Quaker school. What evidence suggests that Banneker received an adequate education?

3. Benjamin Banneker's grandmother, Molly Bannaky, left her own country against her will. Do you think she sympathized with the slaves who were brought to North America? What evidence in her life story shows this?

4. Banneker wrote a letter to President Thomas Jefferson because Jefferson owned slaves. What would give a man whose grandfather and father were slaves the courage to write a letter to the president.

5. If you were to write a letter to any president in the history of this country or to our current president, what would you say? Explain.

Research Topics

Research one of the following African American inventors. Include information about the inventor, his or her invention, what need precipitated the invention, and the importance of the invention. What would life have been like then and what would life be like now without it?

George Alcorn	Henry Blair
Archie Alexander	Sarah Boone
Andrew Jackson Beard	Henry Boyd

Otis Boykin	Jan Ernst Matzeliger
Sarah Breedlowe	Benjamin Montgomery
James Forten	Garrett Morgan
Sarah Goode	Norbert Rillieux
Lloyd Augustus Hall	Lewis Temple
William Hinton	Madame C. J. Walker
Percy Julian	Granville Woods
Lewis Latimer	

My Name Is York.
Elizabeth Van Steenwyk. Illustrated by Bill Farnsworth.
Flagstaff, AZ: Rising Moon, 1997.

African slave York sails and explores with Lewis and Clark on their legendary expedition west. As he journeys through forests and high plains with Lewis, Clark, and Sacagawea and her infant son, York explores his dream of freedom. (*Objet trouve:* miniature compass or smooth stone)

Reader Response Opportunity

Graphic Organizer

Make a Venn diagram showing the similarities between York's life and Sacagawea's life.

Open-Ended Response Opportunity

1. In what ways are York and Sacagawea alike?
2. Captain Lewis and Captain Clark say, "There is no room for dreaming" on the journey into the unknown. York still carries his dream of freedom with him? In your opinion, who is right about dreams, York or Clark? Do dreams get in the way of achieving goals?
3. The Lewis and Clark expedition finally finds a waterway to the western sea. It is a great day for York when he traces his name on the large pine tree. How do you think York feels when he sees and traces his own name on the tree?
4. The Sioux and Shoshones respect Captain Clark as a fair man. Do you think he is fair to York?

NOVEL SELECTIONS

Letters from a Slave Girl.
Mary E. Lyons.
New York: Aladdin Books, 1992.

Winner of the Golden Kite Award; ALA Notable Book.

Harriet Ann Jacobs is a young girl who inherits her mistress's broken promise of freedom. Harriet flees slavery and the advances of her master, and she survives to later write *Incidents in the*

Life of a Slave Girl. Author Mary Lyons bases her book on the life and autobiographical writings of Harriet Jacobs.

Reader Response Opportunity

1. In September 1828 Harriet says, "My dream is done" (Lyons, 42). How is her dream done?
2. Joseph tells Harriet, "The poverty and hardship of freedom [is] always better than slavery." What does this mean to you? Do you think this is true?
3. How does Harriet's life compare to that of Anne Frank? Cite similarities and differences.

Visual Representation: Reward Poster

Have students look at the poster on page 89 offering a $100 reward for the return of Harriet.

1. What types of advertisements does this reward poster resemble?
2. What would an accurate description of you for a missing poster or reward poster say?
3. Create a milk carton advertisement or America's Most Wanted poster for Harriet.

NONFICTION SELECTIONS

Rebels Against Slavery: American Slave Revolts.
Patricia C. McKissack and Frederick L. McKissack.
New York: Scholastic Inc., 1996.

1997 Coretta Scott King Honor Book.

The inherent nature of humankind has made slavery and oppression as old as history. When men and women became slaves to their brothers and sisters, dreams, plans, and plots for liberation began. The McKissacks discuss the many rebels, plans, rebellions, and traitors in the African Americans' freedom campaign.

Reader Response Opportunity

Graphic Organizer

Make a timeline of the rebellions and planned uprisings in the New World from 1492 through the 1880s.

Selected Response Opportunity

Rebels: Select a rebel against slavery from the following list. Identify the person. What did he or she do to attempt to end slavery? What were the results?

Richard Allen	Joseph Cinque
John Brown	Cudjoe
Cato	Henry Highland Garnet
Henri Christophe	Josiah Henson

John Horse	John B. Russwurm
Octave Johnson	Harriet Tubman
Osceola	Nat Turner
Toussaint L'Ouverture	Denmark Vesey
Gabriel Prosser	David Walker

Rebellions: Select an event from the following list and briefly describe it and the chief persons involved.

Denmark Vesey's Uprising	Nat Turner Revolt
Gabriel Prosser's Revolt	Night of Fire
John Brown's Raid	Stono Rebellion

Lest We Forget: The Passage from Africa to Slavery and Emancipation.
Velma Maia Thomas. Photographs and documents from the Black Holocaust Exhibit.
New York: Crown Publishers, 1997.

Beginning with a 1450 map of Africa before the European invasion and culminating with slavery's broken chains, this compelling three-dimensional presentation of the African American experience from Africa to emancipation evokes personal and painful emotions. See the changing face of the African continent. Look into a slave ship's hull and imagine it packed with 600 frightened men, women, and children. Scan advertisements, newspapers articles, and letters that reduce human beings to chattel. Hold in your hands a replica of the Emancipation Proclamation. Pay homage to the millions of enslaved Americans.

Reader Response Opportunity

1. Divide the class into groups of two to four students each.
2. Give each group a removable document or realia from the book. Removable items include a route map to the Slave Coast, a receipt for purchasing a slave, freedom papers, and President Abraham Lincoln's Emancipation Proclamation.
3. Allot a period of twenty-five to thirty minutes for each group to examine their item, discuss their reactions to it, and prepare a group presentation for the class. What does the item reveal about the time and people? Do we have any items today that are similar to it? Explain.
4. Limit group presentations to three to seven minutes.
5. Each group presentation should involve all group members. Presentations can be visual, oral, musical, or adapted to address any other intelligence or learning style.
6. After group presentations allow groups to exchange items and pass around the book to view the other items.

The Narrative of the Life of Frederick Douglass.
Frederick Douglass.
New York: Dover, 1995 (First published in 1845).

Douglass gives an eyewitness account of vicious beatings, slave songs sung in sorrow, families torn asunder, and crushed spirits.

Reader Response Opportunity

1. Douglass learns to value education after he hears his master scold his wife for teaching Douglass his ABCs. Why do you think masters prohibited their slaves from learning to read and write?

2. Douglass argues that the slaveholding religion is hypocritical. What hypocritical policies and practices do we have in the United States today? Explain.

MULTIMEDIA

Glory (video).
Columbia/Tristar Studios, 1989.

Edited for educational use, this award-winning film directed by Steven Spielberg relates the true story of the 54th Regiment, the first all-African American regiment in the Civil War, led by Colonel Shaw. Shaw and the troops constantly battled ignorance and hostility from other Union soldiers and officers. Letter writing took a front seat as Shaw constantly wrote his parents and petitioned influential people on behalf of his troops. This two-hour movie will take more than one class period to show, but the time will be well spent.

The 54th Regiment/Buffalo Soldiers.
http://www.nps.gov/boaf/site1.htm (Search words: *54th Regiment*).

This site offers information, timelines, photographs, recruiting posters, and casualty lists.

The Buffalo Soldiers.
http://www.buffalosoldiers.net.

The Buffalo Soldiers on the Western Frontier.
http://www.imh.org/imh/buf/buftoc.html.

shadowsoldier.org.
http://www.shadowsoldier.wilderness.net.

These Buffalo Soldier sites offer a wealth of information about the United States Colored Troops who came to be known as the Buffalo Soldiers.

Reader Response Opportunity

1. Colonel Shaw told a critic of the "colored regiment" that fighting takes more than physical strength: "there's character and strength of heart." What characters in *Glory* demonstrate these two qualities?

2. The twentieth-century military was segregated for a while. Research the history of African Americans in the United States military and make a timeline detailing it.

3. Did the bravery and success of the Buffalo Soldiers change some people's attitudes toward African Americans? Explain.

4. How do you think integration in the military affected race relations in the United States? Explain.

5. Research Project/Paper: The students will research the 54th Regiment or any of the Buffalo Soldiers and create a mini-project and a short research paper.

WRITING PROMPTS

Elementary Writing Prompt

In the folktale about the pygmy goat and the lion, both animals end up in the trap when the hunter returns.

Write about things that trap people or get them in trouble.

Secondary Writing Prompt

Colonel Shaw wrote to his parents and asked them to appeal to President Abraham Lincoln to allow the 54th Colored Regiment to fight in the Civil War instead of just doing manual labor.

Write a letter to the president or a government official about a policy you believe is wrong.

Multilevel Writing Prompt

Benjamin Banneker wrote a letter to President Thomas Jefferson against the hypocrisy of slavery.

Write about hypocrisy.

7
▼▼▼▼▼

Somebody's Knockin':
Emancipation and Reconstruction

Unless you call out, who will open the door?
—Ethiopian proverb

Somebody's Knocking at Your Door

Somebody's knocking at your door.
Somebody's knocking at your door
Oh-oh, sinner, why don't you answer?
Somebody's knocking at your door

Somebody's knocking at your door (Must be Jesus).
Somebody's knocking at your door (Must be Jesus).
Oh-oh, sinner, why don't you answer?
Somebody's knocking at your door.

HISTORICAL CONTEXT

As Amos Fortune declares in *Amos Fortune: Free Man,* "It does a man no good to be free until he learns how to live . . ." (Yates, 162; See chapter 2, Novel Selections, in this book). The men, women, and children forcibly brought to the United States from Africa knocked at freedom's door from the moment captors snatched them from the cradle of their birth. For far too long, freedom, shackled by a harsh, indifferent government, refused to answer. The liberation African Americans yearned for and sought with vigilance proved elusive for almost 300 years.

The onset of the Civil War and the election of President Abraham Lincoln did not grant swift liberty for slaves, nor did emancipation establish full enfranchisement for ex-slaves. President Lincoln halted several efforts to emancipate slaves during the Civil War. General Benjamin Franklin Butler of the Union Army declared fugitive slaves "contraband of war." Lincoln and Union General John C. Fremont haggled over declaring disloyal owners' slaves free in Missouri. Lincoln and his Secretary of War disagreed over wording in an annual report promoting emancipation. General David Hunter, an abolitionist, and Lincoln clashed over the issue of freeing slaves in three Southern states.

Then, on July 22, 1862, Lincoln advised his cabinet of his plan to free the slaves in the rebel states. In September 1862, the President issued his Preliminary Emancipation Proclamation, to go into effect on January 1, 1863. After an intolerable expanse of years in bondage, freedom shifted from the dominion of the impossible to the realm of reality for the enslaved African Americans of America's South. On January 1, 1863, Lincoln issued his limited Proclamation freeing all slaves in most of the Confederate states.

However, the signing of the Emancipation Proclamation failed to trigger swift improvements for enslaved Africans in America. Most slaves did not receive news of their liberation until months after the effective date of emancipation. The good news did not reach slaves in Texas until June 19, 1865, two and a half years later. Slaves in Tennessee and in parts of Louisiana and Virginia did not gain their freedom from the Emancipation Proclamation. Ultimately, on December 18, 1865, the Thirteenth Amendment abolished slavery in all of the United States (*Freedmen and Southern Society Project*). With the passage of the Civil Rights Act of 1866, Black Americans' rights in the United States seemed protected for all time.

The new liberty of African Americans, emancipation without empowerment, created fresh challenges for a broken nation and for its recently freed men and women. Some were fated to continue laboring for the same masters for minimal pay. Like the Hebrew children in bondage in Egypt, newly freed men and women seemed condemned to making bricks without straw as they toiled on their former owners' land as sharecroppers. The War Department formed the Bureau of Refugees, Freedmen and Abandoned Lands to handle problems brought about by the war, to provide land and provisions for refugees, but no bureaucracy existed to prepare Black Americans and White Americans for their new relationship. No bureaucracy could prepare former oppressors to live side by side with those they once sought to master. For almost a century after the Emancipation Proclamation, African Americans weathered the Reconstruction era, the Great Depression, and Jim Crow laws, unceasingly pursuing the American dream.

MIND MIXER: THOUGHT COMPLETION

1. Students will complete the thought "Freedom is_____."
2. Let volunteers share and explain their answers.

VOCABULARY

alleged	Great Depression	mulatto
assault	homesteader	provisions
biracial	hominy	Reconstruction
blight	Jim Crow	retribution
bureaucracy	jubilee	righteous
cassava	liberian	sharecropper
commemorate	liberty	wit
empowerment	make amends	Zion
fawn (noun)	minimal	

FOLKLORE

A Little Bit of Earth
(Inspired by African American sharecropper tales)

▼▼▼▼▼

Listen, Brothers and Sisters, while I tell you the story of Brother Rabbit and Brother Fox. After the winds of time had blown away the scent of gunpowder and the Union struggled to heal from its gaping wounds, Brother Rabbit and Brother Fox played at being neighbors. Brother Rabbit longed for a small patch of earth to call his own. Poor and homeless as a motherless fawn but full of wit, Brother Rabbit set out to strike a deal with old Brother Fox. Brother Fox, plum full of himself, considered himself the richest and wisest farmer thereabouts. Shortly after sunup Brother Rabbit came upon Brother Fox looking out over his acres of vegetables waiting to be harvested.

"How life treating you this fine day, Sir? Sure look like you got your work cut out for you with all this here," Brother Rabbit's eyes swept across the ripe fields.

"How do, Rabbit? I believe this is the biggest crop I've had in a while," Brother Fox boasted.

"Hope you get all your potatoes in before they rot. Pity you don't have no sons. Yes, Sir! Why if I didn't have to work my own land, I'd be mighty glad to help you!" Brother Rabbit said, shaking his head as he left to work in his imaginary field.

The following morning before the sun had started its day's work, Brother Rabbit again passed by Brother Fox's place. Brother Fox painstakingly broke the ground to loosen his precious potatoes.

"Morning, Brother Fox. Hope life is treating you all right, Sir. I hear tell potato rot took most of Brother Bear's potato crop. Pity you don't have no help! Well, I best be getting home." Bent over in the damp, dark soil, Brother Fox merely nodded and resumed his lonely work.

After breakfast the third day, Brother Rabbit once more happened to pass by the Fox farm as Brother Fox labored in the moist soil.

"Greetings, Brother Fox. See you have plenty more rows of potatoes still need digging. Brother Tortoise says potato bugs ate all of Brother Bear's potatoes. Pity you got to work this land of yours all by yourself!"

"How do, Rabbit? I could use another pair of hands here. Figure I could pay you to help me bring in my potatoes?"

"I got a full crop of corn on my own little farm needs chopping. Sorry I can't oblige you, Sir," Brother Rabbit prepared to leave.

"Wait, Brother Rabbit. If you help me bring in all my potatoes, I will give you as many potatoes as you can eat."

"While I work your land, Sir, the corn and cabbage on my own pitiful farm will rot. I'm not particularly fond of potatoes. Now if you could see fit to give me just a teeny scrap of your farmland, I'd be more than happy to bring in your potatoes and eat just the tops."

"Give you a piece of my land? Why this land has been in the Fox family for more than a hundred years!" Brother Fox hollered.

"Well, then, Sir, best of luck to you. Brother Tortoise say a great rain is coming in a few days that will wash your potatoes right out the ground. Pity you don't have no help."

Day after day Brother Rabbit stopped by Brother Fox's place with news of the blight, potato bugs, potato rot, and foul weather. So in this manner, Brother Rabbit wore down Brother Fox and finally got his very own little bit of earth.

Reader Response Opportunity

1. Complete a Folklore Chart.
2. What strategy does Brother Rabbit use to convince Brother Fox to give him a piece of land?
3. List the advantages and disadvantages of sharecropping as opposed to slavery.

TRADITIONAL LIBERIAN FOODFARE

A dominant food in Liberia, the republic founded by freed African American slaves in the nineteenth century, is rice—rice bread, Jollof rice, check rice. Rice serves as a staple for the majority of Liberian meals, with a meat or seafood entrée of pigs' feet, fish, or shrimp, a vegetable of collard greens, cabbage, or okra with, perhaps, the addition of bananas, sweet potatoes, or cassava, and a beverage of ginger beer.

Reader Response Opportunity

1. Research Liberian foods and recipes.
2. Research dining in Liberia.
3. Locate a recipe for Jollof rice, check rice, or Liberian rice bread.
   Suggested site:

   http://www.sas.upenn.edu/African_Studies/Cookbook/Liberia.html.
   (Search: *Liberia: Menus and Recipes*).
4. What American influences do you note in Liberian culture, including popular food dishes?
5. Write a composition telling how to set the table for a Liberian dinner.
6. Write an explanatory composition telling how to prepare a Liberian rice dish.

PICTURE BOOK SELECTIONS

Freedom's Gifts: A Juneteenth Story.
Valerie Wilson Wesley. Illustrated by Sharon Wilson.
New York: Simon & Schuster, 1997.

On Juneteenth 1943, two cousins, one from New York and the other from Texas, hear a first-hand account of the day African Americans in Texas learned of their emancipation. With soft colors and the storytelling of Great-great-aunt Marshall, a celebration of heritage and history takes on meaning for the girls and for the reader. (*Object trouve:* Texas shape)

Reader Response Opportunity

Prewriting Strategy: Brainstorming

As a class, brainstorm the possible reasons for the two-and-a-half-year delay before Texas slaves learned of the Emancipation Proclamation.

Graphic Organizer

Make a Venn diagram showing the similarities and differences between Independence Day and Juneteenth.

Open-Ended Response Opportunity

1. What is the most important lesson June and Lillie learn from Great-great-aunt Marshall? Why?
2. What valuable lessons can people learn if they take time to listen to older family members?
3. In your opinion, what is the most likely reason the slaves in Texas did not learn that Lincoln had signed the Emancipation Proclamation until two and a half years later?

Ma Dear's Aprons.
Patricia C. McKissack. Illustrated by Floyd Cooper.
New York: Aladdin Books, 1997.

American Bookseller Pick of the Lists; Notable Children's Trade Book in the Field of Social Studies.

In rural Alabama in the early 1900s, a young boy keeps track of the days of the week by the color of the apron his mother wears as she performs domestic chores for others. This book brings to life the self-respect, strength, and hard-working spirit of many single African American mothers then and now. (*Objet trouve:* miniature clothespins)

Reader Response Opportunity

Graphic Organizer

Make a seven-day calendar showing the week's activities for Ma Dear and her son David Earl.

Open-Ended Response Opportunity

1. (Primary/Elementary) What is Ma Dear like? How can you tell? (Grades 6–12) What can you tell about Ma Dear from her actions in the book? Explain.
2. (Grades 6–12): What is the most effective symbolism, imagery, or figurative language McKissack uses in the story? Explain.
3. (Grades 6–12): How is Ma Dear's life different from a single mother's life today?

A School for Pompey Walker.
Michael Rosen. Illustrated by Aminah Brenda Lynn Robinson.
San Diego, CA: Harcourt Brace, 1995.

In 1923 in Madisonville, Ohio, ninety-year-old Pompey Walker recounts his life's story at the dedication of a school to him. Pompey, a runaway slave, and Jeremiah Walker, the son-in-law of a slave owner and from the same plantation as Pompey, raised money for a school for ex-slaves, Sweet Freedom, by repeatedly tricking slave buyers and sellers. This storybook will require several days to read aloud. (*Objet trouve:* school house or school bell)

Reader Response Opportunity

Graphic Organizer

Make a Bio Graph of Pompey Walker's life.

Open-Ended Response Opportunity

1. How are Pompey and Jeremiah's lives similar?
2. Pompey believes his relationship with Jeremiah is "the one true friendship [he] was ever blessed with." What elements of true friendship do you see in the story?
3. Is school/education important to Pompey Walker? How do you know?
4. Has the value of education changed today? How? Why?

Picking Peas for a Penny.
Angela Medearis. Illustrated by Charles Shaw.
New York: Scholastic Inc., 1990.

This simple, rhythmic story reveals a family working the land and celebrating together during the 1930s. Hard, hot work becomes play as the children anticipate the weekly Saturday shopping trip into town. (*Objet trouve:* a penny or a dried pea)

Reader Response Opportunity

Prewriting Strategy: Journal Writing

Write for 5 to 7 minutes about the value of a penny.

Open-Ended Response Opportunity

1. What can you tell about this family from the story? Explain.
2. How has the value of money changed since the time of this story? Explain.

3. (Secondary): How does the rhythm and rhyme of this book affect the tone/mood? Explain.

4. (Secondary): What poetic devices does the author use in *Picking Peas for a Penny*? Do these devices make the story better? How?

I Have Heard of a Land.
Joyce Carol Thomas. Illustrated by Floyd Cooper.
New York, NY: HarperCollins, 1998.

Coretta Scott King Award.

With rich sensory images and powerful figurative language, Joyce Carol Thomas, a National Book Award-honored author, tells of a land full of promise and the people strong and determined enough to claim it for their own. With the deep, earthtone illustrations of Floyd Cooper, renown for his work in children's literature, *I Have Heard of a Land* portrays a single, African American female homesteader as she works the land to make a life for herself. (*Objet trouve:* hominy)

Reader Response Opportunity

1. List everything the reader can learn about Oklahoma from this book.

2. List and explain five examples of figurative language in the book.

3. The author's chosen title for the book, *I Have Heard of a Land,* is also the first line of the hymn "Never grow Old" by James C. Moore. The hymn speaks of the Promised Land, Heaven. In what ways was Oklahoma a promised land?

NOVEL SELECTION

The Land.
Mildred D. Taylor.
New York: Penguin, 2001.

2002 Coretta Scott King Award.

This novel is billed as a prequel to Taylor's 1976 Newbery Medal Novel, *Roll of Thunder, Hear My Cry*. In it, the biracial grandfather of Cassie Logan, *Roll of Thunder*'s main character, fights Reconstruction-era racism from both blacks and whites to build a future for himself and acquire his own land. The author does not sugarcoat the racism and hatred so prepare students for harsh usage of the "n" word.

Reader Response Opportunity

Prewriting/Graphic Organizer

1. Students record their reflections on the novel as they hear or read it. Reflections may focus on character development or the relationship between the two brothers or between the mulatto son and his white father.

2. Make a timeline of Paul-Edward's life.

3. Make a Bio Graph showing the evolution of the relationship between Paul and Mitchell or between Paul and any member of his family.

Open-Ended Response Opportunity

1. Critics have objected to racially offensive language used by characters in *The Land*. Is such language necessary to tell the story? Why or why not?

2. Sometimes when Paul and Mister Edward are alone, Mister Edward calls Paul "Paul-Edward." Paul always addresses his father as "Mister Edward," not "Daddy." How important are the names people call us?

3. How does Paul's relationship with Caroline affect his choices in life?

4. Mister Edward, Paul's father, thinks the skill of carpentry will ensure Paul's success in life. Paul believes owning a plot of land will complete him. What evidence in *The Land* supports both men?

5. Numerous African American landowners in the South had their land taken from them. In some cases, their descendants have attempted to recover the land. In your opinion, what should be done to make amends? Should reparations be made? Explain.

NONFICTION SELECTIONS

Juneteenth: Freedom Day.
Muriel Miller Branch. Photographs by Willis Branch.
New York: Cobblehill, 1998.

Black-and-white photographs and expository text follow the celebration of Juneteenth. From its joyful birth in 1865, an unplanned Texas celebration has evolved into a well-planned, countrywide commemoration of freedom and ethnic pride. Muriel Miller Branch and photographer-husband, Willis Branch escort the reader on a guided tour across the United States. Branch states, "Juneteenth has grown from a mere whisper . . . to a loud shout . . ." (35). From family picnics, hayrides, and turkey shoots to parades, protests, and Civil War reenactments, African Americans set aside a day to honor freedom.

Reader Response Opportunity

1. Make a timeline or Cycle Graph showing the path toward making Juneteenth a recognized holiday.
2. Write a newspaper article or journal entry about the first Juneteenth.
3. If you could recommend a new holiday, what would you suggest? Why?

Freedom's Children: The Passage from Emancipation to the Great Migration.
Velma Maia Thomas.
New York: Crown Publishers, 2000.

Freedom's Children brings black-and-white and sepia photographs, documents, and realia about the life of post-Emancipation African Americans into the hands of its readers. This three-dimensional interactive collection brings today's children and emancipation's beneficiaries together. Suggested read-aloud excerpts:

1. Read to the class excerpts from "Getting to Know Freedom," pages 2–3.
2. Read the advertisement "Information Wanted" on page 2.
3. Read excerpts from the reader on page 6.

Reader Response Opportunity

1. Divide the class into groups of 2 to 4 students each.
2. Give each group a different removable document or realia from the book. Items include a Freedmen's Bureau agent's letter, a land grant, script money, a broadside from an illustrated newspaper, a Colorado & Southern Railway routing ticket, excerpts from a news article and from a letter about an African American farming settlement in Colorado, a secret letter suggesting unequal treatment for African American soldiers during World War I, and documentation of the National Association of Colored Women.
3. Allot 25 to 30 minutes for each group to examine its item and to prepare a group presentation for the class explaining it.
4. As the students meet in their groups, pass the book from group to group, allowing students to examine the photographs and *Freedom's Children*'s immovable items.
5. The presentation should involve all group members, and it should not only explain the document or realia but also give the group's reflections on it. What does the item reveal about the time and people? How does it differ from what we see today?
6. Limit presentations to 3 to 7 minutes.

The Souls of Black Folk.
W. E. B. Du Bois.
New York: Dover, 1994 (First published in 1903)

This unabridged collection of 14 essays interspersed with sorrow songs attests to the strength and dignity of African Americans and foreshadows the protests of the Civil Rights Movement.

Reading Communities

1. Let students select an essay to read.
2. After students have independently read the selected essays, place the students in literary groups based on the essay they have read.
3. In these groups students will discuss the essay they have read.
4. Next, shift students to different groups so that several essays are represented in each group.
5. Students will take turns summarizing the essays they have read.

Reader Response Opportunity

Open-Ended Response Opportunity

Do any of Du Bois's views resemble those of contemporary public figures? Explain.

Composition

Select one essay from *The Souls of Black Folks*. Write a composition explaining the essay. Discuss and defend your opinion of the author's views.

MULTIMEDIA

Reconstruction & Segregation (Video).
Schlessinger Media, 1996.

This 30-minute documentary examines the period following emancipation.

Reader Response Opportunity

Use a Venn diagram to compare and contrast any one of the following pairs:

- Reconstruction era and slavery
- The plight of former slaves after the Civil War and that of former slave owners
- Emancipation of the slaves and the liberation of concentration camp survivors

Juneteenth.
http://www.juneteenth.com.
(Search word: *Juneteenth*).

This Web site explains the history of the Texas Emancipation commemoration that has endured from the nineteenth century to the twenty-first century and has spread from rural Texas to other cities across the United States to celebrate African American history.

Reader Response Opportunity

1. Why do you think Juneteenth continues to have significance among some African Americans in Texas and across the United States?
2. Research Emancipation Day celebrations across the United States. Does any other state have a commemoration similar or equal to the Texas Juneteenth celebrations? Explain.
3. On January 1, 1980, Juneteenth became a legal holiday in Texas, and state employees have the option of taking off on Juneteenth. Should Emancipation Day be a national holiday? Explain.

Oklahoma-at-a-Glance.
http://www.okcareertech.org/ipr/ataglanc.htm.

True to its name, this site gives factual information about Oklahoma and relates the story of Oklahoma's origins. The Web site addresses the diverse cultural subgroups of Oklahoma: outlaws, cattlemen, settlers, Native Americans, cowboys, and African Americans.

Reader Response Opportunity

1. Make a timeline showing the history of African Americans in the Oklahoma Territory.

2. Make a Venn diagram comparing the history of Native Americans and African Americans in Oklahoma Territory.

3. Research famous African Americans who lived in Oklahoma, such as Bill Pickett, Ralph Ellison, or the Buffalo Soldiers (9th and 10th Calvary) and create a mini-project reflecting key information and interesting tidbits.

4. Research the Battle of Honey Springs.

Tulsa Riot of 1921.
Alice Lovelace.
http://www.inmotionmagazine.com/tulsa.
http://www.tulsareparations.

These sites present the story of the Tulsa Riot of 1921 and its impact on African Americans in Oklahoma. African Americans did not always encounter hope and happiness in the "black promised land" of Oklahoma. The Ku Klux Klan and a spirit of supremacy and vengeance threatened the livelihood and very lives of African Americans. The sites chronicle the chain of events leading to the Tulsa Riot, which were disturbing not because of their uniqueness but because so many similar atrocities on both small and grand scales took place around this country after Emancipation.

Reader Response Opportunity

1. Make a timeline of the Tulsa Riot of 1921.

2. Research the twenty-seven African American communities/towns of Oklahoma.

3. Select one community for your focus.

4. Make a Bio Graph showing the highs and lows in this town's history.

5. Write a brief history of the community.

The Rosewood Report.
http://www.freenet.scri.fsu.edu/doc/rosewood.txt.
Remembering Rosewood.
http://www.displaysforschools.com/rosewood.html.
"Sweet Home Rosewood: Lost in the Fire."
Charles Flowers, *The Seminole Tribune,* 20 (39).
http://www.seminoletribe.com/tribune/99/may/rosewood.shtml.
"Is Singleton's Movie a Scandal or a Black 'Schindler's List'?"
Charles Flowers, *The Seminole Tribune,* 20 (4).
http://www.seminoletribe.com/tribune/97/mar/rosewood.shtml.

The Rosewood sites tell the facts and oral tradition behind the disastrous Rosewood Incident. Like the Tulsa Riot, an alleged assault by an African American male precipitated an unleashing of violent retribution against an entire African American community. The events of the Rosewood Incident in January 1923 have chilling similarities to the events that led to the destruction of the community of Greenwood in the Tulsa Riot of 1921.

Reader Response Opportunity

1. Make a T-chart showing the similarities and differences between the Rosewood Incident and the Tulsa Riot.
2. Write an essay comparing and contrasting the two events.

> *The Freedmen's Bureau Online.*
> http://www.freedmensbureau.com.
> (Search words: *Freedmen Bureau* or *Reconstruction*).
>
> *Jim Crow Laws.*
> http://www.afroamhistory.about.com/cs/jimcrowlaws-.
> (Search word: *Jim Crow laws*).
>
> www.cagle.com.
> http://elections.harpweek.com.
> (Search words: *Political cartoons*).
>
> Additional suggested sites:
> *Afro-American Almanac.*
> http://www.toptags.com/aama.
>
> *African American Odyssey.*
> http://www.memory.loc.gov/aaohtml/aohome.html.

Reader Response Opportunity

Have students research one of the above sites and write:

- a newspaper article about the Emancipation Proclamation
- a newspaper article announcing the end of the Civil War
- a commentary/editorial about the end of the Civil War
- a journal/diary entry of an emancipated African American
- a journal/diary entry reflecting on living with the Jim Crow laws
- a newspaper article announcing a Jim Crow law
- a newspaper article covering a violation of a Jim Crow statute
- an editorial column on Reconstruction
- a political cartoon about Reconstruction, the Freedmen's Bureau, Jim Crow Laws, or the Emancipation Proclamation

WRITING PROMPTS

Elementary Writing Prompt 1

Rice is a food often eaten at Liberian meals. Also, cassava and fufu make up part of many West African meals.

> Write about an important food in many meals in the United States.

Elementary Writing Prompt 2

After the Civil War, African American children were free to learn to read, write, and go to school.

> Write about finally getting to do something you always wanted to do.

Secondary Writing Prompt 1

Our families, friends, coworkers, the people whom we choose to love, affect our lives in a variety of ways.

> Write a composition about how relationships shape our lives.

Secondary Writing Prompt 2

Some people use offensive words and revert to name-calling because of their prejudices, ignorance, hostilities, or their own low self-esteem.

> Write about the effect of name-calling and offensive words.

Secondary Writing Prompt 3

The Emancipation Proclamation and the Civil Rights Act of 1866 changed the status of African Americans. The changes did not make everything right for African Americans.

> Write about a change that has both positive and negative consequences.

Multilevel Writing Prompt 1

Around the world at holidays, people often enjoy special foods.

Write about the role of food in culture.

Multilevel Writing Prompt 2

Descendants of former African American slaves commemorate the reading of the Emancipation Proclamation in Texas after the Civil War. Descendants of Holocaust victims strive to ensure that the world never forgets the inhumanities Jews suffered at the Nazi's hands. Native Americans struggle to preserve their history.

Write about the importance of remembering history.

8
▼▼▼▼

The Walls of Jericho: The Civil Rights Movement

Equality is difficult, but superiority is painful.

—African proverb

Joshua Fought the Battle of Jericho

Joshua fought the battle of Jericho, Jericho, Jericho.
Joshua fought the battle of Jericho,
And the walls came tumbling down.
Joshua fought the battle of Jericho, Jericho, Jericho.
Joshua fought the battle of Jericho,
And the walls came tumbling down.

You can talk about a man named Gideon.
You can talk about your king named Saul.
There's none like a man named Joshua,
At the battle of Jericho.

Joshua fought the battle of Jericho, Jericho, Jericho.
Joshua fought the battle of Jericho,
And the walls came tumbling down.

HISTORICAL CONTEXT

At the height of glory and power for the Egyptian empire, the Israelites suffered under the anvil of bondage and oppression in Egypt land. After 300 years the God of Jacob and Joseph heeded the groans of His people and began the process of redeeming Israel. God appointed an unlikely spokesperson to issue His Emancipation Proclamation. From the ranks of the oppressed, He called stuttering, hot-tempered Moses to lead the Hebrew people out of Egypt. Forty years later, after an agonizing journey that was characterized by whining and whishy-washy faith, only two men, Joshua and Caleb, prove faithful and refused to see the giants in their way. With the fortified city of Jericho before them, God issued strange fighting orders: march around the city for seven days; on the seventh day, march around the city seven times. Miraculously, the city fell into the Israelites' hands.

The Civil Rights advocates of the 1950s and 1960s received similar, unorthodox marching instructions and brought about the collapse of the mighty walls of Jim Crow with boycotts, court cases, marches, voter registration drives, and other forms of nonviolent protest. New Joshuas and Calebs arose who refused to acknowledge the giants: Thurgood Marshall, Dr. Martin Luther King, Jr., Ralph Abernathy, Rosa Parks, and many others.

MIND MIXER: WALL OF RIGHTS

1. Complete the following sentence starter: "The most important right to me is_____."
2. Why is this the main right without which you could not live?
3. In small groups of 2 to 4 students, share your answers.
4. On butcher paper let a student list the rights named.
5. Keep the butcher paper posted in the classroom as a "Wall of Rights."

VOCABULARY

apartheid	integration	prejudice
bigotry	Jim Crow	protest
boycott	judicial	restoration
desegregation	legislation	segregation
demonstration	milestone	turbulent
equality	nonviolent	unorthodox
integrate	pacifist	

FOLKLORE

Kiboko, Kifaru, and Sungura the Trickster Hare
(Inspired by African tug-of-war tales)

▼▼▼▼▼

South of the Sahara, when Kiboko, a hippopotamus, and Kifaru, a rhinoceros, had free roam on the vast East African countryside, Sungura the Trickster Hare set out to get the hippopotamus and rhinoceros in the same river at the same time. Sungura the Hare caught sight of his first prey, Kiboko the Hippo, cooling herself in the muddy river waters.

"*Shikamoo*, Mama Kiboko, how are you this fine day?"

"*Marahabaa,* Sungura! The sun burns hotter than the lava that flows from Mount Kenya. Thankfully I only have to share this river with my own kind," Kiboko grumbled. "Now why do you bother me, Sungura?"

"Miss Kiboko, everyone knows the hippopotamus stands as a giant among all living animals, but I believe I can pull you into the river with some little bit of thought and effort," boasted Hare.

"Ha! You pull me into the river. I should like to see that. Why, the Egyptians of ancient days worshipped my great-great-grandmothers while your ancestors simmered in cooking pots surrounded by onions, ginger, yams, groundnuts, and cassava leaves!" bellowed Kiboko the Hippo. "You could scarcely uproot a gourd from the ground."

"Well, then, mighty Kiboko, shall we meet at the south side of the river at dusk and settle this matter for all time," challenged Hare.

"Indeed, at dusk," Kiboko yawned in agreement as she sauntered off to sun herself on the nearest sandbank.

His work only half done, Sungura the Trickster Hare spared no time in searching for Kifaru the Great White Rhinoceros. Sungura easily located Kifaru the Rhinoceros resting beneath a tall baobab tree not far from his favorite watering hole.

"*Hujambo,* Mister Kifaru! What a scorcher we are experiencing today! I took a drink of water from Mama Kiboko's river and the water evaporated before I could swallow it. Speaking of Mama Kiboko, only a few minutes ago she remarked that she is the greatest animal in all the land."

"*Sijambo,* Sungura! That river does not belong to Big Mouth Mama Hippo. I simply prefer not to wade in waters muddied by her kind. With my two horns and strength I could easily dispense of that dim-witted, webbed-toed river hog!" grunted Kifaru.

"Really? Earlier today Kiboko declared herself the strongest animal on the savannah, stronger than Tembo the Elephant and mightier than any two-horned, square-lipped, lazy rhino," taunted the Trickster. "Indeed she even challenged me to a contest of strength and almost won."

"Almost won! What contest? I demand to know," asserted Kifaru. "How could Kiboko possibly think she is stronger than I?"

"Well, Kiboko insisted that she could pull me into the river. Several times I felt myself sliding closer and closer to the water's edge, but Kiboko tired much sooner than I. What a huge splash she made plunging into the water!" Trickster Hare falsely reported.

"The river! I would sooner have my hide pierced by a hunter's spear than go into the muddy river that filthy, insignificant, ill-tempered beast calls home," Kifaru the Rhino said with bitterness.

"Oh, right. Of course, if you are truly stronger than she is, you will pull me into the river quicker than mud dries on your back in the hot afternoon sun."

"Fine, let me dispel any doubts about my power. When and where shall we meet, Brother Hare?"

"Let us meet at the north side of the river after the sun has gone down. Go well, *rafiki.*"

At dusk Kiboko the Hippo met Sungura the Trickster Hare on the south side of the riverbank. Sungura the Trickster gave Kiboko her end of the rope and told her to wait until he reached the other side of the river and pulled on the rope. Then Hare ran to the north side to greet Faru the Great White Rhino.

"Grab the rope. When you feel a tug, the contest has begun." Hare rushed to the middle of the river and tugged on the rope from the south and from the north until Hippo and Rhino began to pull against each other. Hippo swam to the center of the river, kicked and grunted, and pulled and grunted, amazed at Hare's incredible strength concealed in such a wiry body. Kifaru the Great White Rhino, exhausted on the opposite side of the riverbank, refused to admit defeat to the hare. Kiboko and Faru pulled, puffed, and rested, pulled, puffed and rested, until they both slid down their respective sides of the riverbank into the center of the riverbed. As Kifaru bumped into a huge mass beneath the water, he cried out, "Hare, is that you? You are much bigger and stronger than you look on land."

"Kifaru, is that you? Why I never thought you and I would be in the river at the same time! Where is Sungura the Hare? That trickster, his scheming brought us here!" Kiboko answered as she climbed up the riverbank with Kifaru close behind.

"Yes, Sungura has gotten the best of us today. Go well, Friend Faru."

"Stay well, Kiboko," Kifaru bid in farewell, and the two went on their separate ways.

On the riverbank Sungura the Trickster watched, smiled, and hurried away, his ruse successful. Since that day Rhino and Hippo rarely occupy the river at the same time, but Rhino sometimes quenches his thirst in Kiboko's river. Also, in the cool that falls after the sun has bedded for the night, the patient observer will note Mama Kiboko grazing near Faru's grassy home.

▼▼▼▼▼

One classic conflict found in African and African American folktales is the feat of strength or endurance between rivals: a race or a tug-of-war, like the one between the hippopotamus and the rhinoceros. These tales inevitably prove the importance of wit over physical prowess.

"Kiboko, Kifaru, and Sungura the Trickster Hare" has its setting in East Africa, possibly Kenya or Tanzania, rather than West Africa. West Africa typically hosts only the rare pygmy hippo, an unworthy opponent for the mammoth rhinoceros. Ancient Egyptians revered the female hippopotamus. The white rhinoceros ranks second to the elephant as the largest land animal alive, with the river hippopotamus following in third place. At one time the river hippopotamus made its home in rivers throughout the continent of Africa.

Kiswahili Translations

hujambo: casual greeting

kiboko: hippopotamus

kifaru/faru: rhinoceros

marahabaa: response to greeting of respect

rafiki: friend

shikamoo: greeting of respect from a younger person to an older

sijambo: greeting response opportunity

sungura: hare

tembo: elephant

Reader Response Opportunity

1. Make a Cycle Graph for "Kiboko, Kifaru, and Sungura the Trickster Hare."
2. What personality faults do you see in Hippo, Hare, and Rhinoceros?
3. What moral could you write for this tale? Explain.

TRADITIONAL KENYAN FOOD FARE

Kenya, Mecca of safari enthusiasts, has foods as distinctive as the endangered animals foreign travelers come to shoot with guns and cameras: *irio, ugali, ugi, mataha, ndzi, m'chuzi wa kuku, karanga, m'baazi, samaki na nazi, samosas, chapatis,* and *giteke.* Pea beans, groundnuts, coconut, bananas, yams, and fish or chicken often take a central role in Kenyan meals. Served in calabash bowls, groundnut soup is as familiar as Campbell's Chicken Noodle Soup. Three Kenyan mainstays parallel American southern foods. *Uji* and *ugali* of cornmeal mush or gruel complete a Kenyan meal as grits do for many African Americans and southern Americans of all origins. As Africans enslaved in America boiled field greens not worthy of the plantation owners' tables, Kenyans prepare *sukuma wiki,* leafy greens steamed in a beefy sauce. While barbecue for Americans usually means burgers, brisket, chicken, or ribs, Kenyans prefer barbecuing goat or beef. *Chai,* or tea, is not only a major export of Kenya but also a favorite beverage for any time of day.

Reader Response Opportunity

1. Research Kenyan foods and eating customs. Research the Kenyan foods named in this section. Suggested sites:

   All Things Kenyan.
   http://www.allthingskenyan.com/food-.

   African Studies Cookbook.
   http://www.sas.upenn.edu/African_Studies/Cookbook/kenya.html.

   The Congo Cookbook.
   http://www.congocookbook.com.

2. Describe a Kenyan food and compare/contrast it to an American food.

3. Compare and contrast Kenyan and Senegalese eating habits, customs, etc.

4. Write a how-to/explanatory composition on preparing a Kenyan dish.

PICTURE BOOK SELECTIONS

Freedom Summer.
Deborah Wiles. Illustrated by Jerome Lagarrigue.
New York: Atheneum Books, 2001.

In *Freedom Summer* the innocent, honest friendship of two young boys collides with the ignorant, harsh hand of hatred. The 1964 Civil Rights Act changed the laws but not the rigid southern way of life for Joe and for John Henry, son of the woman who cooks and cleans house for Joe's family. Inseparable, Joe and John Henry shell butter beans together, shoot marbles, sweep the porch, chase cats, eat ice pops, and dive into Fiddler's Creek. Yet, the boys' enthusiasm for celebrating by swimming together in the city pool wilts under the blistering presence of unrelenting bigotry.

Reader Response Opportunity

Prewriting: Graphic Organizer

Make a Venn diagram or T-chart comparing John Henry and Joe.

Open-Ended Response Opportunity

1. What figurative language and images does the author use to describe John Henry and Joe?

2. In what way do the two friends experience the benefits of the Civil Rights Act?

Sister Anne's Hands.
Marybeth Lorbiecki. Illustrated by K. Wendy Popp.
New York: Dial Books for Young Readers, 1998.

With humor, button counting, stark reality, hand clapping, garden painting, foot stomping, singing, and a wide-open heart, an African American nun gives her second-grade students a look at the world outside of their parochial lives. (*Objet trouve:* hands)

Reader Response Opportunity

Visual Representation

1. Give students disposable gloves and have them list on the gloves with a fine-tip marker the images drawn from the book, for example, "a paper airplane."
2. Try the same activity on a traced outline of students' hands.

Graphic Organizer

1. Make a cluster/web showing all the characteristics of Sister Anne.
2. Make a cluster/web showing the traits of Anna Zabrocky.
3. Make a Venn diagram showing the similarities and differences between Sister Anne and little Anna.

Open-Ended Response Opportunity

1. What sensory images does the author use to describe Sister Anne and her student, Anna Zabrocky?
2. What figurative language does the author use? In your opinion, which is the most effective example of figurative language in the story? Why?
3. Write a brief description of a teacher who changed your life. Try to use original images and figurative language in your description. What specific traits, actions, and incidents make this teacher notable?

Dear Willie Rudd.
Libba Moore Gray. Illustrated by Peter M. Fiore.
New York: Simon & Schuster, 1993.

The sun sets on a gorgeous Georgia day. Bees buzz in the abelias, mourning doves coo a woeful sound, and the essence of magnolias permeates the air. Fifty-something Miss Elizabeth sits on her porch in her grandmother's wicker chair and rocks and remembers. She remembers Miss Willie Rudd and unmerited slights, indignities, injustices, unspoken thanks, and unfinished deeds. Miss Elizabeth writes a letter of reconciliation to the housekeeper, nanny, and companion of her childhood and, after signing it, folds it into a kite and airmails it skyward. (*Objet trouve:* kite)

Reader Response Opportunity

Write a letter to a person from your past or from history telling him or her something you always wanted to say but never could in person.

NOVEL SELECTIONS

The Watsons Go to Birmingham—1963.
Christopher Paul Curtis.
New York: Delacorte Press, 1995.

Newbery Honor Book; Coretta Scott King Honor Book; ALA Best Book for Young Adults; ALA Notable Book.

The Watsons have the ingredients of the typical all-American family, including two loving parents, sibling rivalry, tattling, 10-year-old Kenny, a rebellious 13-year-old boy, a pampered kid sister, and a trip to Grandma's. However, the Watsons have dark skin, the year is 1963, and the family travels to Birmingham, Alabama. The author tickles us with hilarious family moments and knocks the wind out of us with heartwrenching reality.

Reader Response Opportunity

Graphic Organizer/Prewriting Strategy

1. Make a timeline showing important events in 1963 for the Watsons.
2. Create a comic strip or make a visual representation of any one event in the novel.

Open-Ended Response Opportunity

1. What other historical or recent events remind you of the church bombing in Birmingham? Explain.
2. How does the Watson family change after their trip to Birmingham? Be specific.

Just Like Martin.
Ossie Davis.
New York: Simon & Schuster, 1992.

NCSS-CBC Notable Children's Trade Book.

In August 1963, young Isaac Stone wants nothing more than to follow in the footsteps of Dr. Martin Luther King, Jr. to Washington, D.C., and go to Morehouse College, in nonviolence. Because of his father's objections, Isaac bids his church folks and friends good-bye as they board the busses and then watches the march on television. The euphoria of the church and town in the aftermath of the historic march on Washington abruptly modulates to disbelief and despair after a bomb explodes in the Young People's Bible Class and kills and wounds Isaac's peers and friends. This novel beautifully depicts the chaos and courage of the 1960s.

Reader Response Opportunity

Graphic Organizers

1. Make a Cycle Graph showing the events that lead up to the Children's March.
2. Make a Ring Graph showing the events at the Children's March that lead to Isaac's daddy's arrest.

Open-Ended Response Opportunity

1. How does the author, Ossie Davis, make this story seem as if it really happened?

2. How does Isaac's father change from the beginning of the book to the end? Give specific details to support your answer.

3. Describe the relationship between Isaac, PeeWee, and Dorasthena.

4. What do these three young people have in common?

5. What does Isaac's continual correcting of his own and his friend's mistakes in using the English language tell the reader about Isaac?

NONFICTION SELECTIONS

I Have a Dream.
Dr. Martin Luther King, Jr.. Foreword by Coretta Scott King.
New York: Scholastic Inc., 1997 (Speech—August 28, 1963).

NAACP Image Award.

Fifteen captivating illustrations by Coretta Scott King award-winning illustrators accompany Dr. King's historic speech in a book worthy of any library or bookshelf.

Reader Response Opportunity

Visual Representation

Draw a picture or a symbol reflecting your feelings and thoughts about Dr. King's dream.

Open-Ended Response Opportunity

1. What is your favorite part of the "I Have a Dream" speech? Why?

2. How does the speech make you feel? Explain.

3. What dreams/hopes do you have for the United States and for the world? Explain.

4. Dr. King's "I Have a Dream" speech at the March on Washington has been hailed as a landmark in the history of the United States. In your opinion, how important was this speech to the Civil Rights Movement? What other important speeches have shaped the history of our country? Explain.

5. What figurative language does Dr. King use? Which figurative language do you find most effective? Why?

6. What visual images does Dr. King create? What is his most powerful visual image? Why?

7. What historic references does Dr. King make in his speech?

8. Are Abraham Lincoln and Dr. Martin Luther King, Jr.'s views, actions, and lives similar? Explain.

9. In what ways has Dr. King's dream of racial equality come true? In what ways has it not yet come true? Explain.

My Brother Martin: A Sister Remembers.
Christine King Farris. Illustrated by Chris Soentpiet.
New York: Simon & Schuster, 2002.

In poetic form Dr. King's older sister shares her memories of growing up in the King household. Christine King's childhood reminiscences bring the Civil Rights hero down to earth and portray a flesh and blood child who has his heart broken and his mind confounded by inexplicable prejudices and injustices.

Reader Response Opportunity

1. List life-altering (life-changing) moments from your childhood.

2. Select one memory and make a web showing everything you remember about the experience (emotions, sensory details, actions, reactions, and thoughts).

3. Write about your selected memory.

Through My Eyes.
Ruby Bridges.
New York: Scholastic Inc., 1999.

The Story of Ruby Bridges.
Robert Coles. Illustrated by George Ford.
New York: Scholastic Inc., 1995.

Through My Eyes takes the reader through angry, threatening crowds, up the steps of William Frantz Public School in Mississippi, down deserted halls, and into an isolated classroom for seven months. Ruby Bridges recounts her story with the simple, honest, nonjudgmental manner of a child. The accompanying photographs and interviews create a compelling story.

Child psychiatrist and Pulitzer Prize-winner (journalism) Robert Coles presents a third-person narrative, *The Story of Ruby Bridges,* telling Ruby's story—from her birth to hardworking sharecropper parents in Mississippi to her harrowing experience as a six-year-old girl starting first grade while angry mobs protested, federal marshals guarded, and the world watched from their living room sofas and arm chairs.

Reader Response Opportunity

Prewriting: Graphic

1. On a T-chart list the pros and cons of Ruby's integrating William Frantz Public School.

2. Make a Ring Graph depicting the main events of Ruby's story.

3. Make a Venn diagram comparing and contrasting the two accounts.

Open-Ended Response Opportunity

1. Ruby has learned to obey her parents, which helps her get through first grade. When and how has obeying your parents helped you?

2. People from across America send Ruby gifts, but Ruby's mother makes Ruby share them with her sister and brothers. Is this fair? Why?

3. Ruby has younger brothers and a sister, and this is one reason her mother feels Ruby has to integrate William Frantz Public School. Do you think it is fair for older children to have the responsibility of their younger siblings placed on their shoulders? Explain.

4. Ruby believes that she lost her childhood the year she integrated William Frantz Public School. What events in her story might make her feel this way?

5. Ruby Bridges gives an honest, first-hand account of her experiences. How do you think Ruby's story can help others?

6. How does Coles' book differ from Ruby Bridges' book?

7. Which version helps you better understand what happened? Why?

Children of the Dream: Our Own Stories of Growing Up Black in America.
Laurel Holliday.
New York: Pocket Books, 1999.

In *Children of the Dream,* part of the international *Children of Conflict* series, thirty-eight African American writers give their personal accounts of growing up in the last half of the twentieth-century in America. The black-and-white photographs of the writers in their youth give faces to the words. Each writer's painfully realistic recollections remind the reader of the many unknown casualties of the Civil Rights Movement.

Reader Response Opportunity

1. Write questions to ask an adult about an important time or event in history.

2. Interview a family member or other adult about the Civil Rights Movement or other historical time period in the United States.

3. Record your interview.

4. Write your conclusions of what you learned from the interview.

Warriors Don't Cry.
Melba Patillo Beals.
New York: Archway, 1994.

Congressional Medal.

The author, recipient of a Congressional Medal, shares her personal experiences as one of nine teenagers who integrated Central High School in Little Rock, Arkansas. Beals' diary entries from that time period, UPI, API, and family photographs, and her recollections expose the frightening face of the bully bigotry.

Reader Response Opportunity

Prewriting Strategy

In a reflection log, record thoughts and reactions to the events in Melba's life.

Graphic Organizer

Make a Ring Graph of the events that led to Minnijean's suspension.

Open-Ended Response Opportunity

1. Grandma India advises Melba to counter hostility with cheery politeness. As Melba follows her grandmother's counsel, her attackers seem unsure of how to respond. Do you think answering cruelty with kindness works? Give at least one example to support your opinion.

2. Melba and the others of the Little Rock Nine experience a year that binds them forever in history. What other young people have made a permanent mark on history? Explain.

3. If you had to go through similar circumstances, would you react more like Melba, who combats meanness with forced politeness, or like Minnijean, who retaliates? Explain.

Dear Mrs. Parks: A Dialogue with Today's Youth.
Rosa Parks with Gregory J. Reed.
New York: Lee & Low, 1996.

With gentle strength and humility, Rosa Parks speaks to people of all ages as she answers forty years of letters from children. Mrs. Parks advocates hope, forgiveness, diligence, and courage to continue the pursuit of the dream.

Dear Dr. King: Letters from Today's Children to Dr. Martin Luther King, Jr.
Jan Colbert and Ann McMillan Harms. Photographs by Ernest Withers and Roy Cajero.
New York: Hyperion Books, 1998.

Memphis school children, ages seven through thirteen, write insightful and sincere letters to the martyred Drum Major of Peace. These children of diverse ethnic backgrounds see America for what it is because of King's efforts and for what it can yet become.

Reader Response Opportunity

1. Write a letter to any figure from the Civil Rights Movement asking for his or her opinion about the progress of civil rights since the 1960s.

2. Imagine you are Rosa Parks or Dr. Martin Luther King, Jr. and write an answer to one of the children's letters in the book.

MULTIMEDIA

We Shall Overcome: Historic Places of the Civil Rights Movement.
http://www.cr.nps.gov/nr/travel/civilrights/.
National Register of Historic Places.

This site offers a map and itinerary of forty-nine key places in the Civil Rights Movement.

MLK Page.
http://www.wmich.edu/politics/mlk/.
Western Michigan University, Department of Political Science.

San Diego Union-Tribune Award.

This site consists of a timeline of African Americans' struggle for justice, from *Brown v. Board of Education* to the shattering events of the 1960s. Also included are statements from key figures in the movement.

The History Net: African-American History.
http://afroamhistory.about.com/.

On this site are articles about major events in the Civil Rights Movement, such as the church bombing in Birmingham and the subsequent investigation and trials.

Reader Response Opportunity

Graphic Organizers

1. Make a timeline of the most important events of the Civil Rights Movement in the 1950s and 1960s.
2. Make a Ring Graph of the events that led to the Montgomery Bus Boycott.
3. Make a T-chart listing the pros and cons of affirmative action.
4. Make a Venn diagram showing the similarities between the lives and philosophies of Dr. Martin Luther King, Jr. and Malcolm X.
5. Make a Ring Graph or Cycle Graph showing the sequence of events surrounding the Greensboro sit-ins.

Composition Options

1. Write a composition explaining and supporting your opinion on the merits and constitutionality of affirmative action.
2. Write a composition explaining and supporting your opinion on which is greater, states' rights or federal law.
3. Write a composition, explaining and supporting your opinions, about which man achieved more for African Americans, Malcolm X or Dr. King.
4. Explain and support your opinions on which event is more important in the Civil Rights Movement of the 1950s and 60s: *Brown v. Board of Education*, the Rosa Parks arrest, or the Greensboro sit-ins.

Research

Choose a topic from the list below:

1. Research your topic.
2. Create a PowerPoint presentation, Web page, pamphlet, political cartoon, or other visual representation of your topic.
3. Write a research paper about your topic.

Suggested Topics

Brown v. Board of Education of Topeka, Kansas	Civil Rights Act of 1991
Thurgood Marshall	Greensboro Four
Rosa Parks	Dr. James Farmer
Fred Shuttlesworth	Montgomery Bus Boycott
NAACP	March on Washington 1963
CORE	Freedom rides
Little Rock Nine	Freedom summer
Medgar Evers	SCLC
Sixteenth Baptist Church bombing—Birmingham, Alabama	Ralph Abernathy
SNCC	Fannie Lou Hamer
Stokely Carmichael	James Meredith
Malcolm X	Emmett Till
Civil Rights Act of 1964	Eldridge Cleaver
Voting Acts Right of 1965	Reverend Jesse Jackson
Swann v. Charlotte-Mecklenburg Board of Education.	Vernon E. Jordan
Civil Rights Act of 1968	Julian Bond
Civil Rights Restoration Act	

Additional Suggested Civil Rights Movement Sites

We Shall Overcome: Historic Places of the Civil Rights Movement.
http://www.cr.nps.gov/nr/travel/civilrights/mainmap.htm.

The Civil Rights Movement.
http://school.discovery.com/lessonplans/programs/freeatlast/index.html.

Civil Rights Timeline: Milestones in the Modern Civil Rights Movement.
http://www.infoplease.com/spot/civilrightstimeline1.html.

Civil Rights Movement 1955–1965.
http://www.watson.org/~lisa/blackhistory/civilrights-55-65/.

Greensboro Sit-Ins: Launch of a Civil Rights Movement.
http://www.sitins.com.

Eyes on the Prize: Fighting Back (1957–1962) (Video).
WGBH Educational Foundation and Backside Productions, PBS, 1987.

Fighting Back covers the six-year period during which Americans fast-forward the emancipation process the Confederate South put on pause almost a century earlier. Protestors afraid of change and civil rights advocates weary of the stagnant waters of injustice come together in increasingly volatile encounters, and the world watches.

Skin Deep: The Fight Against Legislated Racism (Video).
WGBH Educational Foundation and the BBC, 1999.

Emmy Award;
Peabody Award.

Skin Deep, a 60-minute educational video narrated by John Forsythe and Alfre Woodard, carries the viewer through the turbulent and dramatic Civil Rights era in the United States and the struggle against apartheid in South Africa. This video shows actual footage from the Civil Rights Movement and interviews with people who experienced the hatred. Racial slurs pepper the video; advise children accordingly. It may be most suitable for secondary and post-secondary audiences.

4 Little Girls (Video).
A Spike Lee Production. HBO Studios, 1997.

This 102-minute video contains interviews and news coverage from the tragic bombing of a church in Birmingham, Alabama, which killed four girls and touched the heart of America.

Reader Response Opportunity

Graphic Organizer

1. Make a timeline of the Civil Rights Movement in the United States.
2. Make a T-chart with one column for South Africa and one for the United States, outlining each land's struggles for equality.

Open-Ended Response Opportunity

1. Do you think the Civil Rights Movement in America has inspired South Africans in their fight for equality? Explain.
2. How has the struggle in South Africa differed from America's?

WRITING PROMPTS

Elementary Writing Prompt

Throughout history special people have managed to remain calm and nonviolent in spite of what they suffered.

Write about staying peaceful when bad things happen.

Secondary Writing Prompt 1

Dr. Martin Luther King, Jr. and the freedom fighters practiced nonviolent civil disobedience, just as Mahatma Gandi did in India.

Write about using peaceful methods to bring about change.

Secondary Writing Prompt 2

According to the Ashanti proverb, "There is no medicine to cure hatred." The success of the Civil Rights Movement did not alter the hearts and minds of many Americans accustomed to the Jim Crow way of life.

Write about the influence of hatred.

Multilevel Writing Prompt

"Tell me whom you love, and I'll tell you who you are," declares an African American proverb.

Write about the importance of the friends and loved ones whom we choose.

9
▼▼▼▼▼

That Old Time Religion: Spiritual Heritage

The man who remembers others remembers also his Creator.
—Nigerian proverb

Give Me that Old Time Religion

Give me that old time religion.
Give me that old time religion.
Give me that old time religion.
It's good enough for me.

It was good for the Hebrew children.
It was good for the Hebrew children.
It was good for the Hebrew children.
It's good enough for me.

It was good for dear old Daniel.
It was good for dear old Daniel.
It was good for dear old Daniel.
It's good enough for me.

It was good for Paul and Silas.
It was good for Paul and Silas.
It was good for Paul and Silas.
It's good enough for me.

It was good for my dear mother.
It was good for my dear mother.
It was good for my dear mother.
It's good enough for me.

It was good for my dear father.
It was good for my dear father.
It was good for my dear father.
It's good enough for me.

Give me that old time religion.
Give me that old time religion.
Give me that old time religion.
It's good enough for me.

HISTORICAL CONTEXT

Just as the River Nile flows through northeast Africa into the Mediterranean Sea, old time religion stretches across Africa's history and spills over into the continuing narrative of Africa's plundered progeny. Since the moment in eternity when God Elohim expelled Adam and Eve from Eden's Paradise Garden in a state of fallen grace, the kingdoms, tribes, and nations of Africa, along with civilizations around the world, have religiously inclined their ears toward the heavens, hoping to hear from their disgruntled landlord, the Supreme God.

Elohim, Nyame, Aondo, Olorun, Imana, Obassi Osaw, Lisa, Ngewo-wa, Moomb, Amma, Mantis, Pemba, Dxui, Alo, Abassi, Chiuke, Famien, Asase Ya, Sango, Dugbo, and the ancestors— the inestimable list of deities and spirits among the indigenous, polytheistic religions of Africa rivals the number of oral languages spoken on the African continent. A host of demigods who govern the sky, the sun, the moon, crops, weather phenomena, the underworld, death, fire, fertility, the sea, diseases, war, evil, and benevolence receive homage. Long before Judaism, Christianity, and Islam entered the pageantry of African life, a multiplicity of indigenous religious beliefs and practices defined and directed the lives of Africa's sons and daughters.

In the fullness of time, Yahweh and Jesus the Christ competed with Islam's Muhammad for African souls. A growing collection of evidence from Biblical writings, historical records, legend, tradition, and scientific data points to the presence of Judaism, Christianity, and Islam on the African continent prior to the onslaught of the Atlantic slave trade. Biblical references to Africa and Africans can be found in Genesis, the first book of the Old Testament, as the passionate love affair between Yahweh and His people commences in the Garden of Eden and continues in the New Testament, as related in the events of the life of Jesus Christ and His maiden bride, the first century A.D. Christian church.

The Israelites repeatedly passed through fertile Canaanland to and from Egypt. Abraham, patriarch of faith for both Jews and Christians, sojourned in Egypt with his kinfolk to escape famine. Deceived by Abraham, the Egyptian Pharaoh took Sarah, Abraham's beautiful wife, into his house. After the God of Abraham sent plagues to Pharaoh's house, Pharaoh cast Abraham and his people out of Egypt. Three generations later Abraham's great-grandsons sold their favored brother, Joseph, into slavery. In Egypt the Lord God of Abraham, Isaac, and Jacob promoted Joseph from the lowly state of slave to advisor to Pharoah and used him to save the Egyptians and the descendants of Abraham from yet another devastating famine.

"Now there arose a new king over Egypt, which knew not Joseph" (Exodus 1:8). Once again, as in the days of Abraham, the Israelites fell from favor, their transgression this time prosperity and fertility. Amid the mystery of a fiery, fireproof bush, the eternal I AM THAT I AM (Exodus 3:14) commissioned Moses, the adopted Israelite grandson of the Pharaoh, to return to Egypt and deliver the multitude of Hebrews from bondage. The prophet Jeremiah wrote of Israelites escaping to Egypt when the Babylonians conquered Israel. Egypt, blessing and curse. Jehovah God's chosen people found sanctuary among this great African civilization in seasons of hunger and in times of peril.

In addition to Biblical references to Africa and its people, African and European oral tradition, written documents, and scientific research suggest a Judeo-Christian presence on the African continent before the onset of the African Diaspora. Medieval legends speak of the mythical African Catholic king and priest, Prester John. Historians also recount the lives of Askia Muhammad, a faithful Muslim, and Affonse I, an African king who converted to Christianity. Established African Jewish communities make their homes in Egypt, Libya, Ethiopia, Tunisia, and Algeria (*African Jew*, 2002). Results of DNA testing on members of the South African Lemba tribe have enhanced their claim of being the descendants of Aaron, the brother of Moses. The tribe's adherence to Jewish customs and dietary practices substantiate their claim to Judaism perhaps dating back to the time of King Solomon.

Ethiopian folklore recognizes King Solomon, known for his legendary wisdom and for building a temple for the Lord, as the ancestor of all Ethiopian kings. Ethiopian legend and the ancient Jewish historian Flavius claim that the Queen of Sheba who visited King Solomon (I Kings 10) was the Queen of Egypt and Ethiopia. Ethiopian kings descend from Menelik, the son of King Solomon and the Queen of Sheba.

Down forty-two generations of Abraham's lineage, Jesus, the son of God, arrived on the scene wrapped in swaddling cloths, heralded by angels and worshipped by shepherds. Perhaps the magi bearing gifts of gold from afar to the infant Jesus followed the star from Africa's Gold Coast. The God who delivered Israel from Egypt sent His only son, Jesus, into exile in Egypt to flee Herod's soldiers. Roman soldiers called upon Simon of Niger to carry the cross of Jesus the Christ on the road to Golgotha. On the road from Jerusalem to Gaza, the apostle Phillip evangelized and baptized an Ethiopian eunuch who was on his way home to Ethiopia.

Religion served as a multiedged sword for non-Africans making decisions regarding the livelihood of Africans. Asian and European invaders disguised their desire for wealth beneath a cloak of evangelism, spreading the Islamic and Christian faiths while accumulating land and riches for their kings and queens. European Americans in favor of slavery cited the Old Testament as evidence of Africans' cursed status as descendants of Ham and claimed the Bible endorsed slavery. Abolitionists adhered to Christ's teachings of "Love thy neighbor . . ." (Matthew 19:19) and "Preach deliverance to the captives . . . set at liberty them that are bruised" (Luke 4:18). Enslaved Africans drew hope and strength from stories of those who were in impossible situations but prevailed: faithful Noah surviving the flood, aged Abraham fathering an heir, fugitive Moses facing a powerful Pharaoh, Joseph the favored son ruling over his brothers, David the shepherd boy slaying a giant Goliath, Daniel escaping the lion's mouth, the three Hebrew men fireproof in a fiery furnace, Jesus and a borrowed tomb. Choosing to live by faith and not by sight, a great number of America's black bondservants adopted the religion of those who enslaved them, seeking deliverance from a just, benevolent God.

Though stripped of their material belongings, kidnapped West Africans did not disembark on the American continent bereft of spiritual resources. These men, women, and children had centuries of ancestors to call upon, a tradition of fervent worship, and an abundant spiritual heritage on which to build. The marriage of the joyful fervor of traditional African religious practices like the circle dance, praise songs, and call-and-response chants to the European and New World faith produced robust offspring, the African American church. Lost lambs far from home and in need of a benevolent shepherd, many Africans in America found hope in the ancient story of the intimate relationship between a chosen, oppressed people and a faithful, omnipresent, and omnipotent deliverer. At the beginning of slavery, the pursuit of religion by Africans in the American colonies received little encouragement or support. Ignorance, prejudice, a need for control, and fear often discouraged European Americans from allowing African Americans to worship freely.

The African American church has a long-standing reputation for not only ministering to the soul but also for involving itself in political and social concerns. Since emancipation the African American church has evolved from a clandestine link in the Underground Railroad to an active twenty-first century. Reconstruction African American preachers, often the only literate African Americans in the community, climbed to positions of political power. Many churches also performed double duty as schoolhouses. During the Civil Rights Movement a century later, African American preachers again took leadership roles. African American churches and their pastors spearheaded the Civil Rights Movement by rallying folks in the church house. Many leaders came from the ranks of ordained preachers. In sizzling Freedom Summer, African American churches prepared civil rights gladiators of many faiths to enter the stadium against the lion of racism and let God fight their battles. Even today African American churches promote voter registration, local political candidates show up at Sunday service before municipal elections, and community churches serve as polling stations. In the twenty-first century, membership in African American churches booms. African American souls find meaning and redemption in Christianity, Islam, Jehovah's Witness, Rastafarianism, spiritualism, and mysticism.

From the mysticism of the exported West African religions to the rhetoric of Dr. Martin Luther King, Malcolm X, Louis Farrakhan, and Reverend Jesse Jackson, religion weaves throughout the chronicles of African American history like delicate threads in the finest woven *kente* cloth. Captives threw themselves overboard or persevered by drawing from the well of faith in the gods of their ancestors. Ibo men and women imported to the Georgia and Carolina Sea Islands took along their religious practices. Over time their conjuring and their beliefs in the myriad minion deities known as *orishas* intermingled with their newfound Christianity and gave birth to the inimitable Gullah and Geechee customs and religious practices. In the South slave owners and their defenders used the Bible as license to subjugate the African. Quakers and other abolitionists received inspiration to advocate and work for freedom from oppression from the pages of the Holy Bible. Enslaved Africans held secret camp and bush meetings on the land of their oppressors to sustain their faith. African American preachers shepherded wandering freedmen after emancipation.

The African American church is birthmother to rhythm and blues, jazz, and soul music superstars like Aretha Franklin and Whitney Houston. In choir stands and on brutally uncomfortable wooden church pews with thin, crimson cushions, budding musicians nurse on a formula of exquisite harmonizing, hand clapping, toe-tapping, and synchronized swaying. Religion as ancient as the Tigris River and as enduring as Egypt's pyramids adorns the royal cloth of African American history.

MIND MIXER: BRAINSTORMING

1. Brainstorm as many religions and denominations as possible.
2. Compare and discuss lists in small student groups of 2 to 4.
3. The groups then compile a composite list.
4. Group representatives share their answers.
5. Record the answers on the board, overhead transparency, or on a large chart tablet.
6. Discuss with the class why they think there are so many different religions, denominations, and beliefs in the world.

VOCABULARY

apostle	Judeo-Christian	proselytize
conjure	messianic	redemption
convert	monotheistic	religious affiliation
deity	mysticism	revere
denomination	pastor	sovereign
evangelize	patriarch	superstition
Genesis	pious	supreme
gladiator	polytheistic	zealot
Islamic		

FOLKLORE

May the King Live Forever
(Based on "No-King-as-God," a Hausa legend of Nigeria)

▼▼▼▼▼

In the ancient Songhai Empire on the West Coast of Africa, the conquering emperor demanded that the newly subdued Hausa people greet him at all times with "May the king live forever." A certain peanut farmer respectfully declined to greet the king in this manner. As zealous and pure of heart as Shadrach, Meshach, and Abednego, Hebrew captives of Babylonian King Nebuchadnezzar, the groundnut farmer refused to bow to any king but God. Each time he came in the presence of King Askia the Conqueror, the farmer nodded his head, clapped his hands, and boldly proclaimed, "There is no king but God. Only God is sovereign." His fellow Hausa neighbors soon begin to call the farmer No-King-but-God.

As you may well imagine, the monarch's anger burned seven times hotter than Nebuchadnezzar's fiery furnace. Yet, desiring the favor of his subjects and wary of offending God, the king hesitated to have No-King-but-God summarily put to death for his passive, steadfast disobedience. Instead King Askia sought advice from Nyamakalaw, the highly revered historian who held the ageless wisdom of the Hausa people in his soul. The royal author told Askia, monarch of the Songhai Empire, of a king greater than he, Obassi Osaw, the supreme deity of the Hausa people. "Even the Niger River must flow around the island, Oh, king. I beg you not to persecute this harmless, pious farmer for his faithfulness to his god. Even the mighty must bend to the will of a higher power."

After meeting with Nyamakalaw, Askia devised a cunning plot to trap the zealous farmer without offending Obassi Osaw, the Hausa god, and awakening his wrath. To put his scheme in place, King Askia wasted no time implementing his plan. He called for his royal messenger.

"Find the peanut farmer the people call No-King-but-God. Instruct him to present himself to me at my palace at the third hour after the sun's rising on the morrow."

The royal messenger swiftly located the farmer in his fields caring for his peanut crop like a lioness tending to her young cubs and delivered the king's message. The following morning at the appointed time, the farmer appeared before King Askia in the royal courtyard. "There is no king but God," the farmer chanted as he bowed his head before Askia.

"No-King-but-God, I see you are a decent, hardworking, honest man. No other man or woman in my kingdom honors God as you do. Because of your upright reputation, I wish to entrust the imperial golden ring to your care. Guard it with your life. I will send for the ring when I have need of it. Our law decrees the citizen who loses the golden ring must die."

No-King-but-God hurriedly returned to his dwelling. He hastened to hide the ring before his young wife, Afua, returned from tending sheep. Afua hungered for exquisite jewelry of gold and silver more than a newborn lamb hungers for its mother's milk. The farmer placed the ring of gold in a goat's horn, spread plantain leaves over the horn, and waited for his wife's arrival.

"Nana Esi saw one of King Askai's messengers near our hut this morning, Husband," Afua remarked on her return as she set about grinding millet.

"There is no king but God, Dear Wife," the humble farmer said in reply.

Curious about the royal visitor and dissatisfied with her husband's response, Afua determined within herself to watch her husband closely. A few plantain leaves at the head of his mat seemed very important to No-King-but-God. Each evening as No-King-but-God returned from caring for his peanut plants he cautiously checked beneath the plantain leaves, shaking the horn to hear the jingling of the king's ring. One morning after the peanut farmer left to tend his crop, Afua ran to the pile of leaves.

"A goat's horn? All this bother for a goat's horn! Surely my husband has gone mad just as the villagers say." Taking the worthless goat horn with her, Afua gathered the pots for water and hurried to the river. At the riverside with the village women, Afua showed Nana Esi the goat's horn.

"Nana Esi, my husband hides this worthless goat horn in our home as if it were an ivory tusk or a priceless jewel. As each day fades into evening, he examines it. A worthless goat's horn! Listen, it has a pebble within it." With contempt Afua tossed the horn into the river.

Fleet feet carried word of No-King-but-God's latest foolishness around the village swifter than the north winds blow red dust across the parched earth, as wives, sisters, daughters, and mothers returned from the Niger River to their own huts. That evening, as was his custom, No-King-but-God lifted the covering of plantain leaves to inspect the hidden treasure. A small gourd lay in place of the goat's horn. Afua swiftly averted her eyes and silently stirred her pot of groundnut stew. At that moment King Askai's messenger appeared at the farmer's door.

"King Askai requests you present yourself at the imperial palace tomorrow morning with the royal ring."

No-King-but-God solemnly nodded in reply.

"Ring?" thought Afua, "The royal ring! Have I flung the imperial ring into the river?"

Neither Afua nor No-King-but-God savored their favorite groundnut stew. Afua's guilt from knowing the penalty for losing the king's ring caused her to sleep fretfully that night. Visions of her poor husband's disgrace and execution paraded before her closed eyes. Not daring to ask Afua about the missing ring, the troubled peanut farmer also spent a restless night. Before Grandfather Moon passed the lighted torch to the rising sun the next morning, No-King-but-God left the hut.

"I shall stop by the river and catch a fine fish to carry to the royal palace. Surely God will provide. There is no king but God. God will provide. There is no king but God," he echoed to no one but himself and God as he made his way to the riverbank. In very little time the faithful farmer caught a large fish in his net. He took the fish and made his way to the palace.

"May the king live forever. King Askai, the foolish farmer has arrived with a fish, Great King," announced the messenger. "I took the liberty of sending the fish to the cook."

"A fish? And where, I wonder, is the ring of gold?" asked King Askia, "Very well. Guards, seize the farmer and bring him to me."

"No-King-but-God, I hear you have brought a fish with you to my courts. Have you perchance changed the imperial ring into a fish?" King Askai inquired derisively.

Before No-King-but-God could answer, the cook ran into the room with the messenger and four guards at his heels. "May the king live forever. Great King Askai, I sliced open the fish that the peanut farmer brought. Inside the fish I found a goat's horn. When I held the horn up by its end, out fell the royal ring. How wise of you Great King to place the ring in this shrewd farmer's care!" the cook exclaimed.

"True wisdom begins in fearing God," the faithful peanut farmer asserted joyfully as he clapped his hands. The king had no choice but to reward the fervent farmer and send him on his way. "There is no king but God," the humble peanut farmer declared as he returned to his shanty.

▼▼▼▼▼

Askia was the name of several kings of the West African Songhai Empire, beginning in 1493 with Askia I, also known as Askia Muhammad or Askia the Great. Askia Muhammad extended the Songhai Empire by capturing the Hausa states and other territories. Askia also refers to the office or position of a Songhai king. Many Hausa have lived in Niger and in northern Nigeria for more than a thousand years. The farmers grow peanuts, millet, peas, sorghum, and manioc. The majority of the Hausa people adhere to Islamic teachings.

Reader Response Opportunity

Prewriting/Graphic Organizer

1. Complete a Folklore Chart on "No-King-but-God."
2. Complete a Cycle Graph on "No-King-but-God."

Open-Ended Response Opportunity

1. In your opinion is the peanut farmer a disloyal subject for refusing to say, "May the king live forever"? Why or why not?
2. Is there ever a time when a person's beliefs should outweigh the laws of the land? Explain your answer.
3. Who is the wisest character in the folktale: the king, the peanut farmer, or the farmer's wife? Why?
4. Do the spiritual "Old Time Religion" and the folktale "May the King Live Forever" have anything in common? Explain.

Research Topics

1. Have students write a specific question they want answered about one of the topics listed below. For example: When did the Hausa first arrive in Nigeria? What are the main foods of the Hausa? How long have the Fulani and the Hausa inhabited Nigeria?
2. Students then research the topic using media and library sources.
3. After researching the topic, students can create a visual with text to demonstrate what they have learned.

Askia I/Askia Muhammad	Lake Chad
The Islamic Faith in the Songhai Empire	The Niger River
Hausa people	Niger
Nyame	Nigeria

TRADITIONAL GROUNDNUT FOOD FARE

Groundnuts, goobers, or groundpeas, by any name this underground pea or fruit is more than a snack to eat at a baseball game. In West Africa groundnuts, or peanut butter, appear in sauces, soups, and stews, and as a main course: groundnut stew, groundnut-seafood soup, groundnuts with rice, groundnut chops, groundnut-tomato sauce, groundnut ice cream, and banana desert sprinkled with chopped groundnuts and other fruits. Senegal boasts the title of groundnut (peanut) capital of the world.

Reader Response Opportunity

1. Research the cultivation and harvesting of peanuts.
2. Research George Washington Carver. How do his peanut products and uses for peanuts compare to West Africa's use of groundnuts?
3. Research African groundnut recipes or African American peanut recipes.

Suggested sites:

http://www.congocookbook.com (Search: *groundnuts* or *peanuts*)

http://www.sas.upenn.edu/African_Studies/Cookbook/cb_spot.html

http://www.co.beaufort.sc.us/bftlib/gullah.htm

http://www.recipesource.com/ethnic/africa/00/rec0006.html

http://www.sas.upenn.edu/African_Studies/Miscellany/Recipes

4. Make a Cycle Graph demonstrating the steps in preparing a groundnut dish.

3. Write a how-to/explanatory composition telling how to prepare a groundnut dish or a George Washington Carver peanut product.

PICTURE BOOK SELECTIONS

The Creation.
James Weldon Johnson. Illustrated by James E. Ransome.
New York: Holiday House, 1994.

Under the shade of a towering tree, a country preacher clad in patched overalls tells creation's story to an attentive circle of youth. The illustrations capture the magnificence of nature: fragile, fluttering, monarch butterflies, spangling stars, hollowed out valleys, flashes of lightning, rolling waters, beasts, birds, and humankind. James Weldon Johnson's writing and James Ransome's art are a glorious match.

Reader Response Opportunity

1. The illustrator offers pastoral scenes of a storyteller under the shade of a tree regaling children, along with bold strokes that depict creation. In your opinion, do the illustrations suit the writing? Support your opinion with specific details.

2. What examples of figurative language does James Weldon Johnson employ? Which example is your favorite? Explain.

3. List some of the imagery James Weldon Johnson uses. Which is the strongest? Why?

Come Sunday.
Nikki Grimes. Illustrated by Michael Bryant.
Grand Rapids, MI: Eerdmans Books for Young Readers, 1996.

Come Sunday starts with a gentle wake-up call on a Sunday morning and ends with the recitation of "The Lord's Prayer" at bedtime. In between rising and resting, the narrator invites the readers to Paradise with blue-haired ladies, high-stepping ushers, collard greens, black-eyed peas, fried chicken, honey-glazed yams, spirit-filled preachers, and a helping of feel-good to take home until the next Sunday.

Reader Response Opportunity

Prewriting Strategy/Graphic Organizer

1. Make a timeline of the young girl's Sunday events.
2. Make a cluster or web showing everything the girl sees and hears in the church on Sunday morning.

Open-Ended Response Opportunity.

1. From the girl's description, which part of Sunday do you think she likes best? Why?
2. What does *Come Sunday* reveal about the religious life of the family in the story?

David's Songs: His Psalms and Their Story.
Colin Eisler. Illustrated by Jerry Pinkney.
New York: Dial Books, 1992.

Contemporary paraphrasing and simple yet elegant illustrations transport the reader to the hillsides and pastureland of King David's time.

Reader Response Opportunity

Prewriting

Make a T-chart or Venn diagram showing the similarities between the prose form of any psalm in the book and in the King James version of the Bible.

Open-Ended Response Opportunity

1. The psalms have long been a favorite for people needing comfort, assurance, or encouragement. Which psalm of those included in *David's Songs* is your favorite? Explain.
2. What imagery and figurative language does the psalmist use in your favorite psalm?
3. The psalmist originally composed the psalms as songs. Today we usually read them as poetry. How are poetry and music similar?

NONFICTION SELECTIONS

Africa.
Yvonne Ayo. Photographs by Ray Moller and Geoff Dann.
New York: Alfred A. Knopf, 1995.

This reference book offers magnificent illustrations and brief explanatory text on facets of life among the diverse nations on the African continent. These sections "Religion and Beliefs," "Myth and Magic," "Medicine and Healing," "A Way of Death," and "Nations at War" demonstrate how religious practice pervades every aspect of life.

Reader Response Opportunity

1. As you read the various sections of this text, you will notice that religion has a hand in almost every aspect of African life. How is the United States similar to or different from the African nations in the influence of religion on everyday life? Give specific examples and details.

2. What has happened in recent or current events that underscores the impact of religious beliefs on our lives?

3. Recurrently the issues of the separation of religion and government and the freedom of religion have arisen in the United States. Do you think it is possible to completely separate religion from government in this country? Explain.

African-American Religion.
Albert Raboteau.
New York: Oxford University Press, 1999.

From West African villages to twentieth-century African American churches, this text examines religion not as a separate entity but as something that is interwoven into the multilayered, multicolored cloth of African American life.

Reader Response Opportunity

Prewriting

1. List major people and events in early African American religious life following Emancipation.

2. Make a timeline that shows the development of African American religion.

Open-Ended Response Opportunity.

It has been said by many that the most segregated hour in the United States is the time of worship. Why do you think most churches in this country are still predominately (and historically) reserved for one ethnic group or another? Is it a matter of color, culture, style of worship, or something else?

God, Dr. Buzzard, and the Bolito Man: A Saltwater Geechee Talks about Life on Sapelo Island.
Cornelia Walker Bailey.
New York: Doubleday, 2000.

As you read Cornelia Walker Bailey's remembrances, you will feel as though you are sitting on a porch drinking a tall glass of iced tea while listening to your great aunt talk about the good old days. In *God, Dr. Buzzard, and the Bolito Man,* Cornelia Walker Bailey takes readers to the water, immersing us in the name of the three-in-one: superstition, Christianity, and conjure.

Reader Response Opportunity

Graphic Organizer

Make a Bio Graph of Cornelia Walker Bailey's life.

Open-Ended Response Opportunity

1. The narrator tells about dying and coming back to life at the age of three. Do you think she really died? Explain.

2. How does this event affect Cornelia's life?

3. Why do you think the traditions and culture of Sapelo Island have survived so long?

4. The author reveals some of the superstitions and religious beliefs on the island. What interesting or unusual superstitions have you heard about in your life?

5. How do you suppose superstitions begin?

6. Describe the author's style of writing. Does her writing reflect her background as a Sea Islander?

MULTIMEDIA

African Christianity: A History of the Christian Church in Africa.
http://www.bethel.edu/~letnie/AfricanChristianity/.

Egypt, Ethiopia, the Congo, Sierra Leone, Uganda, South Africa, and North Africa—the author investigates the genesis and metamorphosis of Roman Catholic and Protestant churches across the African continent.

Divining America.
http://www.nhc.rtp.nc.us.

The nineteenth-century section of *Divining America* examines the influx of African slaves into the United States and the integration of African religious practices with the preexistent religious practices during an era of spiritual awakening in this country. The twentieth-century section looks at Marcus Garvey and the religious components of his Universal Negro Improvement Association in the 1920s. It also examines Islam and African Americans.

Exploring Africa: Christianity in Africa.
http://exploringafrica.matrix.msu.edu/curriculum/lm14/stu_actfour14.html.

This site explores the history of Christianity on the African continent.

The Black Church: Source of Spiritual, Social, Civil Nurture.
Delma J. Francis, 2003.
http://www.startribune.com/stories/614/3637830.html.

Since its founding the African American church has given African Americans a safe haven. In the South slaves met in clandestine, hushed arbors to worship and pray for better days. With the changing needs of African Americans over time, the church has evolved to meet these needs: banquet hall, NAACP meeting place, Civil Rights Movement rallying point, and nucleus of the African American community. *The Black Church* uncovers the vast influence of the African American church.

Reader Response Opportunity

Prewriting

Make a timeline of religion in Africa.

Open-Ended Response Opportunity

1. Many have made the observation that churches are the most segregated places in the United States. Do you agree? Explain.
2. What role do you think the church should play in the twenty-first century?
3. Many call America a Christian nation. Do you think America is truly a Christian nation? Explain.

Research Topics

Research one of the following topics and write an essay, create a PowerPoint presentation, or design a Web page.

1. **The Church and Politics.** Research one of the following African American leaders who had their start in African American churches. Find information on his background, education, and religious affiliation as well as his goals and achievements.

   Nat Turner

   Adam Clayton Powell

   Reverend Jesse Jackson

   Dr. Martin Luther King, Jr.

   Ralph Abernathy

   Louis Farrakhan

   Marcus Garvey

   Father Divine

   Malcolm X

   Omar Ibn Said

   Mohammed Alexander Webb

   Nobel Drew Ali

   Elijah Muhammed

   Reverend Al Sharpton

2. **Significant Events and Movements.** Research these events or movements. Explain their significance in history and their effect on African or African American life.

   Founding of St. Thomas African Episcopal Church, Philadelphia

   Establishment of the National Baptist Convention

   Universal Negro Improvement Association

   Million Man March

   The Moorish Science Temple

   The American Muslim Movement

   The McCarran-Walter Act of 1952

The White Fathers and Holy Ghost Fathers

Church involvement in the Civil Rights Movement

Church burnings

Church bombings

Prewriting

1. Make a timeline of Islam in West Africa.

2. Make a timeline of Christianity in West Africa.

3. Make a Bio Graph showing the fluctuation of church membership in African American churches since Emancipation.

Research Topics

The relationship between Queen Sheba and King Solomon

The South African Lemba tribe

Menelik, son of Queen Sheba and King Solomon

Prester John

Freedmen churches

The African American church during the Civil Rights Movement

Religion on the Georgia and Carolina Sea Islands

Malcolm X

Reverend Jesse Jackson

The African Methodist Episcopal Church

The National Baptist Convention

Rastafarians

Black Jews

Richard Allen, AME Founder

Father Divine

WRITING PROMPTS

Elementary Writing Prompt

Laws in the United States prevent people from praying in school.

> Should children be allowed to pray in school? Why? Write about this.

Secondary Writing Prompt 1

The First Amendment is often cited when people debate prayer in school. Review the First Amendment.

> Write about the First Amendment and prayer in public schools.

Secondary Writing Prompts 2

Frequently the African American church has taken a stand in political and social matters including encouraging voter registration, introducing political candidates, and protesting incidents involving some form of injustice.

> Should churches get involved in politics and community concerns?
> Support your opinion.

Multilevel Writing Prompt

Every ancient culture seems to have had some type of religion.

> Write about the importance of religion.

10
▼▼▼▼▼

Music in the Air: Musical Legacy

For there they that carried us away captive required of us a song...

—Psalm 137:3 (KJV)

Over My Head

Over my head I see trouble in the air
Over my head I see trouble in the air.
Over my head I see trouble in the air.
There must be a God somewhere.

Over my head I see music in the air.
Over my head I see music in the air.
Over my head I see music in the air
There must be a God somewhere.

Over my head I see color in the air.
Over my head I see color in the air.
Over my head I see color in the air.
There must be a God somewhere.

Over my head I see glory in the air.
Over my head I see glory in the air.
Over my head I see glory in the air.
There must be a God somewhere.

HISTORICAL CONTEXT

Whisked away and cruelly enslaved far from their native home like the Israelites in captivity in Babylon, despondent and uprooted Africans learned to "sing the Lord's song[s] in a strange land" (Psalm 137). Corn ditties, cabin songs, plantation melodies, and jubilees, oppression gave birth to this Antebellum African American traditional music. Music gave disenfranchised men and women a voice, with lyrics that proclaimed an eternal home free of tribulation: *Heaven, Jordan, Canaan*, the *Promised Land, Zion*, and the *Campground*.

African American music bears an inimitable mark as distinct as an individual's DNA, yet it is as universal as water. African American music rocks the listener with rhythms that soothe, comfort, inspire, and ignite. Vibrant shades of color in the prism of America's music—spirituals, ragtime, jazz, rhythm and blues, gospel, rock and roll, pop, hip hop, rap, and reggae—developed from the African American experience. The "Who's Who" of African American music includes the Fisk Jubilee Singers, Paul Robeson, Scott Joplin, Eubie Blake, Louis Armstrong, Duke Ellington, Bessie Smith, Marian Anderson, Mahalia Jackson, Thomas Dorsey, Margaret Douroux, B. B. King, Chuck Berry, Nat King Cole, James Brown, Barry Gordy, Aretha Franklin, Stevie Wonder, James Cleveland, Walter Hawkins, Diana Ross and the Supremes, Marvin Gaye, the Temptations, Gladys Knight and the Pips, the Jackson 5, Andrae Crouch, Kirk Franklin, Whitney Houston, and Luther Vandross.

Since the era of the Fisk Jubilee Singers, music connoisseurs in the United States and the world abroad have sampled from the banquet table of African American music, savored the taste, and copied the recipes. In the aftermath of slavery, African American music was welcome in the parlors and automobiles of White Americans while the Black men and women who had shaped the music drank from separate water fountains, entered through the back doors of restaurants, sat in the balconies of movie houses, learned from discarded textbooks with pages missing, and waited for the brighter days of which they sang.

Relentless strains of "Oh, Freedom" and "We Shall Overcome" accompanied Civil Rights activists on the streets, courthouse steps, and across the bridges of the segregated South. Thomas Dorsey's prayerful "Precious Lord" has aroused congregations for decades, provoking tears to fall and holy shouting to erupt. The wide-reaching acceptability of the gospel music recorded by Mahalia Jackson in the 1950s and 60s, in tones richer than Colombia's greatest coffee and with a depth of passion, foretold the monumental success of African American music in the entertainment industry in the twentieth and twenty-first century. Repentant slave ship owner Isaac Watts would perhaps marvel to hear his "Amazing Grace" flow from the mouths of those whose ancestors he conspired to enslave. From Uganda to Nigeria to the Kalahari Desert to the rain forests of Central Africa to Nashville to Motown to Bobby Jones Gospel Hour, booming from automobile stereos and church sound systems, the music of African Americans fills the air.

MIND MIXER: DISCUSSION

A age-old, well-known quote says, "Music hath charms to soothe the savage breast, to soften rocks, or bend a knotted oak" (Congreve, 1729). Discuss your thoughts on the following topics with a partner:

1. Does music have the power to soothe people or in any way change how a person feels?
2. If you believe music is powerful, why do you think it is so powerful?
3. What examples of music's influence have you seen or experienced in real life, in literature, in movies, or on television? Explain.

VOCABULARY

activist	coronation	melody
alto	despondent	pageantry
ambassador	discord	professional
antebellum	ditties	songster
arranger	ensemble	soprano
baritone	expatriate	spiritual
bass	harmony	tenor
chorus	hymn	tribulation
composer	jubilee	unpatriotic
conclave	lyrics	virtue
contralto	melodious	

FOLKLORE

Kintu's Kingdom
(Based on Ugandan fact and folklore)

▼▼▼▼▼

The explosive blast of gunfire, the undeniable noise of booted government storm troopers in the streets, and the clamor of frightened citizens scurrying for safety intensified the sense of urgency Kabaka Sir Edward Mutesa II experienced.

"Quickly, destroy the gongs, the xylophone, the harp, the lutes, the trumpets, and the royal drums before Obote's army arrives. Obote's men must not seize the imperial instruments. God helping me, Obote may take hold of the palace, but he will never control the heart of the kingdom."

These words spoken, Kabaka Mutesa II awaited the imminent demise of the once rich and powerful Buganda Kingdom and reflected on the story of his people's beginnings. Atop a pure white horse, Mutesa had ridden to the coronation site at Naggalabi. Cries of "*Kabaka Yekka. Kabaka Yekka*. Long live Kabaka, the tree under whose shade we peasants stand!" rang out from the throngs of people along the way. The *Lakiko,* the Crown's Council, and the *bitangole,* the king's men, vowed to defend him to the death. Mutesa's heart had overflowed with pride as he listened to the author recite the story of Nnambi, queen, and Kintu, the first *kabaka,* king of Buganda.

Master musicians became one with their instruments as they performed; gong-chimes, harps, drums, trumpets made of ivory tusks, and the xylophone contributed to the pageantry of his coronation. Clad in a ceremonial *kanzu* of the purest white bark cloth, Kabaka Mutesa II had sat upon the throne and listened as words and music chronicled the history of Kato Kintu, Kabaka Chwa, Prince Kimera, Kabaka Mutesa I, Kabaka Mwanga and the proud lineage of the royal clan, the Oluyo Olulangira. The Baganda revered the Kabaka, the sovereign ruler over both body and soul of all the people, the symbol of the goodness and glory of Buganda.

The Ganda people, the Buganda Kingdom, and the Oluyo Olungira royal clan had their beginnings generations before Kabaka Edward Mutesa II assumed power. Long before explorers from across the great waters visited Uganda, a young East African named Kato Kintu arrived from the Nile Valley to the fertile farmland near Victoria Nyanza. With nothing more than his health, strength of mind, a flute fashioned of bamboo, and Ng'ombe, his cow, Kintu hoped to make a life for himself. Kintu played his flute as Ng'ombe grazed in the lush savannah. He harvested bananas and coffee, fished, and hunted. Solitary work greeted Kintu as each day dawned. Night after night loneliness lay next to him as he slept.

Then Nnambi, Princess of the Sky, came to the land of Kintu seeking a husband. The moment Princess Nnambi spotted young Kintu with skin the color of the darkest coffee beans, the strength of ndovu, the elephant, and the courage of ten *simbas,* she set her heart on marrying him. Nnambi returned to her home and told her father, Ggulu, about Kintu. Because Ggulu cherished his daughter and lived to fulfill her every desire, he devised a plan to bring Kintu and Nnambi face to face. He called his son, Kiwanuka, Spirit of Lightning, to his side.

"Nnambi has chosen a husband. Speak to her, and go where she tells you. There you will find an upright, prudent man called Kintu. Steal away his only possession of worth, his cow, and bring it to your father's house. Move slowly. I want the young man to follow you home."

To Ggulu's satisfaction, Kiwanuka completed his task with ease, and Kato Kintu appeared at Ggulu's home in the heavens demanding the return of Ng'ombe, his cow. Anger evaporated like the morning dew as Kintu beheld the stunning Nnambi, lovely as an African violet and graceful as a gazelle. Her hair and body washed in the milk of Kintu's cow, a necklace of cowries around her noble neck, adorned in the finest robe of terra cotta bark cloth, Nnambi conquered Kintu's love. Kintu took Nnambi for his wife amid a grand *ngoma* with the heavenly sounds of bells, drum chimes, gourd drums, the lute, and joyous dancing feet. The two lived in peace and contentment for many days. In the fullness of time, Nnambi gave birth to their healthy first-born son, Kiweewa. *Omuhiire* (Good Fortune) had smiled on Kintu.

Faster than the chicken hawk plucks the chick from the ground, the threat of danger jeopardized Kintu and Nnambi's happiness. Ggulu received word that his eldest son, Walumbe, Spirit of Death, would soon return home from his long journey on earth tormenting the sons of man. Walumbe threatened to kill the man who had married his sister without his approval. "How dare Father give Nnambi in marriage while I was away! Who is this mortal? What bridewealth did this Kintu offer to deserve the hand of Nnambi, the Princess of the Sky?"

Ggulu called Nnambi and Kintu to him. "Pack up quickly and return to Kintu's home. I can no longer guarantee your safety if you stay here. Whatever happens, do not return unless I send Kiwanuka to bid you come. Live in good fortune, my children."

After a hasty, sorrowful farewell, Kintu returned to his farm near Victoria Nyanza with all the bounty he had acquired from his mission: Ng'ombe, his cherished cow, a herd of cattle, guinea fowl, goats, millet, bananas, maize, gold, ivory, the *omutuba* or bark cloth sapling, and his wife, Nnambi. Kintu and Nnambi made a good life on their farm. Nnambi fed the guinea fowl, collected the eggs, milked the cows, gathered the bananas, made cloth from the bark cloth tree, and harvested the maize. Kato Kintu tended his cattle, crafted drums with cow hide covers, and traded bark cloth, ivory, and cattle with travelers for weapons, spices, and silk. Ruhanga (Creator) again blessed Kintu and Nnambi's union with a child.

It seemed *omuhiire* dwelt once again with Kintu and Nnambi. Walumbe's threats and Ggulu's words of warning lost their potency in the wake of Kintu and Nnambi's prosperity. Disregarding her father's parting words of caution, Nnambi returned to her father's house to retrieve the wedding gifts left behind in their haste: coffee beans and millet for her hens. This time as Nnambi journeyed to her new home, Walumbe followed her and confronted Kintu.

"Kato Kintu, you are not worthy of my sister. Give me Kiweewa, your first born, to work for me or illness and death will stalk your family. As the lion sneaks upon the herd of zebras and snatches the weakest from its midst, so shall I steal your children from among you."

Kneeling over the moist soil of his farmland, Kintu squeezed a handful of eucalyptus leaves and let them fall onto the earth. "Let Ruhanga have his divine way. I will never willingly give my sons over to your hands."

Walumbe persisted in his demand, but Kato Kintu and Nnambi held steadfast in their resistance. One by one, Walumbe beckoned his sister's children to their death, first Kiweewa, then the others, but Ruhanga blessed Kintu and Nnambi with more sons and daughters. And so, for more than thirty-five generations, the story of Kintu and Nnambi continued as the descendants of Kintu and Nnambi ruled over the Kingdom of Buganda.

Six hundred years after Kato Kintu breathed life into the Ganda people and created the Kingdom of Buganda, his final successor faced certain exile. Commander Amin's troops seized the palace. The music of Kintu's Kingdom fell silent, except in the souls of its people.

▼▼▼▼▼

Ugandan Facts and Folklore

Ugandan oral tradition speaks of two distinct leading men named Kintu: Kintu, the Adam-Man, and Kato Kintu, Buganda's alpha king. Oral accounts of Ugandan history frequently mesh the two men into one. This telling of the story of "Kintu's Kingdom" purposely pairs Kintu, the first Kabaka, with Nnambi, legendary wife of Kintu, the first man. In East Africa's cradle of civilization, Creator God forms the first human, Kintu, and presents him with a wife, Nnambi. All Ganda people, all humanity, life, marriage, reproduction, and death spring from the union of Kintu, the Adam-Man, and his queen, Nnambi.

Thousands of years later Kato Kintu, forerunner to all *kabakas* of Buganda, appears in the Lake Victoria region, calls a conclave of the clans, and reigns over the new kingdom. Carrying out Apollo Milton Obote's orders, Major Commander Idi Amin's troops storm the palace. The Kingdom of Buganda falls. No longer will a *kabaka* rule over the Baganda people.

Reader Response Opportunity

1. Complete a Folklore Chart or do a Cycle Graph about "Kintu's Kingdom."
2. Make a Venn diagram or T-chart comparing Kato Kintu to another legendary hero.

TRADITIONAL HEAVENLY BANANA FOOD FARE

Musa Paradisiaca, the Heavenly fruit, Potatoes of the Air (Gibbon, 1999), known as *ndizi* in Kiswahili, plantains and bananas appear in a variety of culinary dishes in Africa. The Baganda featured in "Kintu's Kingdom" preferred bananas above other foods as their civilized food. The sky god, Ggulu, offered Kintu and Nnambi bananas or plantains as one of their wedding gifts. Ibn Battuta, a great, Moroccan medieval traveler and author, wrote of a relish containing mangoes, ginger, pickled lemon, and cooked bananas. Five hundred years later Richard Francis Burton, nineteenth-century traveler, encountered plantains in East Africa and described this plant as "The Staff of Savage life" (Gibbon, 1999).

Fry plantains in palm oil, or, for a healthful alternative, boil them in coconut milk. Mash plantains with yams to make fufu. Make beer or wine from plantains. Steam fish, yams, or plantains wrapped in plantain leaves. This heavenly food fed both East Africans and West Africans centuries before Europeans journeymen carried it to Europe and the New World.

Reader Response Opportunity

1. Research African recipes with bananas or plantains as an ingredient. Suggested Web site:
    http://www.congocookbook.com.
    (Search words: *African banana recipes*).

2. Select a recipe, list its ingredients, and make a Cycle Graph chart outlining the steps for preparing the dish.

3. Write a how-to composition explaining how to prepare the recipe. (*Objet trouve:* banana chips)

PICTURE BOOK SELECTIONS

I See the Rhythm.
Toyomi Igus. Illustrated by Michele Wood.
San Francisco: Children's Book Press, 1998.

Coretta Scott King Award.

This brightly colored mural of 500 years of African American music shows its evolution from the drumbeats of Africa to hip hop. The text and art create their own rhythm.

Reader Response Opportunity

1. In what ways can you see and hear rhythm in the lines of this book? Give specific examples of sound devices, sensory images, and figurative language in *I See the Rhythm*. (Elementary: What do you see, hear, and feel when you read this book?)

2. Make a timeline or collage showing the history of African American music.

3. Select a musician, term, music era, or type of music presented in *I See the Rhythm*. Research the topic and write a brief report or prepare a presentation or mini-project to share with the class.

Suggested Research Topics

slave drums	Louis Armstrong	Cotton Club
slave songs	Charles Bolden	Savoy Ballroom
blues	Ferdinand "Jelly Roll" Morton	Ella Fitzgerald
Scott Joplin	Dixieland sounds	boogie woogie
ragtime	swing	Mamie Smith
W. C. Handy	Duke Ellington	Bessie Smith
Bert Williams	Cab Calloway	Billie Holiday
William Grant Still	big band jazz	be bop
jazz	Harlem renaissance	Minton's Playhouse
Storyville	Fletcher Henderson	Thelonious Monk
banjo	Chick Webb	Charlie Parker

Dizzy Gillespie	Gregory Hines	Janet Jackson
Chano Pozo	Mahalia Jackson	Whitney Houston
Miles Davis	Bobby Jones	James Brown
Leontyne Price	Yolanda Adams	Stevie Wonder
Max Roach	Cece Winans	Chuck Berry
John Coltrane	Vickie Winans	Little Richard
Sammy Davis, Jr.	Aretha Franklin	Jimi Hendrix
Clifford Brown Quintet	rhythm and blues	rock 'n' roll
Charles Mingus	Motown Records	Woodstock
gospel	Barry Gordy	funk
Reverend Thomas Andrew Dorsey	Diana Ross	hip hop
Margaret Douroux	Michael Jackson	rap

Lift Every Voice and Sing.
James Weldon Johnson. Introduction by James Haskin. Illustrated by Elizabeth Catlett.
New York: Walker and Company, 1993 (song first copyrighted in 1921).

Written by James Weldon Johnson with music by his younger brother, J. Rosamond Johnson, to commemorate Abraham Lincoln's birthday on February 12, 1900, "Lift Every Voice and Sing" exhorts African diaspora survivors to sing Zion's songs. Austere, black-and-white linocuts accompany this song of faith. "Lift Every Voice and Sing" routinely brings audiences and congregations of Americans of African descent to their feet, and many generations have adopted the hymn as the unofficial African American national anthem. (*Objet trouve:* musical note)

Reader Response Opportunity

1. What figurative language and poetic devices does Johnson employ in "Lift Every Voice and Sing"? Give specific examples.
2. In your opinion, what is the main idea the author tries to communicate with this song?
3. How is "Lift Every Voice and Sing" similar to "The Star Spangled Banner"?
4. "Lift Every Voice and Sing" has been unofficially proclaimed the African American national anthem. Do the words successfully express the experience of African Americans? Explain.

How Sweet the Sound: African-American Songs for Children.
Wade and Cheryl Hudson. Illustrated by Floyd Cooper.
New York: Scholastic, Inc., 1995.

How Sweet the Sound brings together a panorama of music born from the African American experience: traditional spirituals, cakewalk songs, street cries, hymns, freedom songs, children's rhymes, the African American national anthem, and tunes by Stevie Wonder and James Brown. Supplementing the words and music, the Hudsons provide background facts about the origins and composers of the songs, while Floyd Cooper's illustrations enhance them with their gentle shades of browns.

Reader Response Opportunity

1. Name and describe a children's lullaby, rhyme, or clapping rhyme or jump rope chant.
2. What picture would you draw to go with the song or rhyme? Explain.
3. How important is music to children?
4. Select a piece from this book and discuss the poetic devices and figurative language used.

A Band of Angels.
Deborah Hopkinson. Illustrated by Raul Colon.
New York: Aladdin Paperbacks, 2002 (Atheneum, 1999, hardback).

Golden Kite Award; ALA Notable Book; NCTE Notable Book; *Smithsonian Magazine* Notable Book; Publishers Weekly Best Book.

"Sometimes songs arise from happiness, sometimes from sorrow," Aunt Beth tells the young narrator of *A Band of Angels*. Aunt Beth relates the story of the unchainable voices and spirits of the Fisk Jubilee Singers, who for seven years took former slave songs around the United States and Europe to raise funds for Fisk University. (*Objet trouve*: cherub/angel stickers with harps)

Reader Response Opportunity

Graphic Organizer

Make a Bio Graph of Grandma Ella's life with a brief explanation.

Open-Ended Response Opportunity

1. The Fisk Jubilee Singers sang the traditional spirituals that had been cast aside as painful, shameful reminders of slavery. Why do you believe audiences had such an overwhelmingly positive response to this music?
2. Has music impacted race relations in the United States? If yes, how?

Summertime.
Lyrics Composed by George and Ira Gershwin; DuBose and Dorothy Heyward. Illustrated by Mike Wimmer.
New York: Aladdin Books, 1999.

"The livin' is easy"; sunflowers, tire swings, shimmering butterflies, hammocks, front porches, and sultry sunrises full of promise make worthy companions for "Summertime" from *Porgy and Bess*. The reader will thirst for a tall glass of iced tea or lemonade after reading this book. (*Objet trouve:* sunflower or sunflower seed)

Reader Response Opportunity

Graphic Organizer

Make a cluster or web showing all the images of summertime.

Prewriting Strategy

Write a journal entry about your favorite season.

Duke Ellington: The Piano Prince and His Orchestra.
Andrea Davis Pinkney. Illustrated by Brian Pinkney.
New York: Hyperion Books for Children, 1998.

Caldecott Honor Book; Coretta Scott King Award.

Andrea Pinkney's swinging words and Brian Pinkney's swirling paintings are in perfect harmony as they showcase Duke Ellington's talents as well as theirs. The lyrics and rhythm whisk the reader onto the dance floor of the Cotton Club or to a front-row seat at Carnegie Hall to hear the Duke of jazz in person.

Reader Response Opportunity

1. What poetic devices does the author use to describe Duke Ellington's music?
2. What figurative language does the author use?
3. Does the writing help the reader/listener hear or feel music? Explain.
4. How has Duke Ellington influenced American music?

When Marian Sang: The True Recital of Marian Anderson, The Voice of a Century.
Pam Muñoz Ryan. Illustrated by Brian Selznick.
New York: Scholastic Inc., 2002.

Flavors of brown: deep pecan, milk chocolate, creamy peach, butterscotch, russet, toffee, cinnamon, nutmeg, and bittersweet dark chocolate. The range of hues in this book's tasteful illustrations mirrors the depth of the enchanting contralto tones of Marian Anderson, whose voice attracted worldwide audiences. Marian's story, an ample offering of history and song, satisfies the palette.

Reader Response Opportunity

Graphic Organizer

Make a cluster or web showing the positive characteristics of Marian Anderson. Include details to support each trait.

Open-Ended Response Opportunity

1. Why do you think Marian Anderson's singing appeals to people in both Europe and American, regardless of race?
2. Does music break barriers? Explain.

NOVEL SELECTIONS

Bud, Not Buddy.
Christopher Paul Curtis.
New York: Random House, 1999.

Newbery Medal; Coretta Scott King Award.

Ten-year-old Bud, weary of shuffling from one foster home to another, runs away in search of his elusive musician father. The author masterfully weaves humor, harsh reality, and hope into the plot of this award-winning novel.

Reader Response Opportunity

Graphic Organizer

Make a Cycle Graph, Bio Graph, or timeline illustrating the main events of Bud's life.

Prewriting Strategy

Keep a journal recording your daily reflections as you read *Bud, Not Buddy.* Note if any of the experiences in the book remind you of events in your life.

Open-Ended Response Opportunity

1. How does Bud change in the novel?
2. What does Bud learn about life during his search for his father?
3. What does the reader learn about the music scene and life in the United States during Bud's youth? Explain.

NONFICTION SELECTION

The Sweet Hell Inside: A Family History.
Edward Ball.
New York: HarperCollins, 2001.

The story of the Harlestons begins with a plantation master, William Harleston, and a slave girl. This biography, written by the author of the 1998 National Book Award-winning *Slaves in the Family,* tells the story of a gifted, Charleston "high yellow" family. One influential relative, the Reverend Daniel Jenkins, runs a children's home for African American waifs. To generate funds for his orphanage, the "orphanage man" establishes the Jenkins Orphanage Band with discarded band instruments and his promising "black lambs," including several musicians who go on to successful careers in music, meeting up with jazz notables like Duke Ellington, Louis Armstrong, Mamie Smith, and Jelly Roll Morton. The text swells with tidbits of information and insights about "the colored elite," Charleston, and the world of art and music in the 1920s.

Reader Response Opportunity

1. What do the Fisk Jubilee Singers and the Jenkins Orphanage Band have in common? How do the two groups differ?
2. Was it ethical for Reverend Jenkins to have the band perform to earn money for the orphanage? Explain.
3. The author writes about the "high yellow," colored elite. In the twenty-first century is there still preferential treatment for lighter-skinned African Americans? Do other ethnic or racial groups have their own elite? Explain.

4. Make a T-chart or Venn diagram showing the similarities between Oliver Twist's Fagin and Reverend Jenkins.

5. Write an essay comparing Fagin's treatment of waifs to Reverend Jenkins' treatment of his orphans.

MULTIMEDIA

Trying to Get Home: A History of African American Song (Video).
Written by and featuring Kerrigan Black.
Heebie Jeebie Music & Ellison Horne Video, 1993.

In this one-man comprehensive overview, Kerrigan Black guides the viewer through the evolution of African American music. Black masterfully narrates and performs representative African American music, from slave sorrow songs to twentieth-century soul music. The video both enlightens and entertains.

Reader Response Opportunity

Prewriting Activity

Have students record in their journals their feelings and reflections as they view the video and listen to the music.

Graphic Organizer

Have students make a timeline or collage of African American music, using the information gleaned from the video.

1. Research one of the musicians mentioned in the video.

2. Research the music of a specific sub-Saharan African culture. Describe the music of the culture and explain the role of music in the culture.

3. Research one of the following instruments or musical traditions and its history in Africa:

baakisimba	friction drum	master drum
body percussion	gong	musical bow
choral music	gong-chimes	oboe
clapper	harp	rattle
drum	Hausa algaita	soukous
drum chimes	hocketting	talking drum
empuunyi	idiophones	trumpet
endingidi	iron bell	xalam
engalabi	lamellaphone/mbira	xylophone
ensaasi	lute/kora	zither
flute		

The American Experience: The Jubilee Singers (Video).
Produced by Llewellyn Smith and Andrew Ware.
WGBH with Nashville Public Television.
PBS Video, 1999–2000.
http://www.pbs.org/wgbh/amex/singers/.

Braving racial, social, and financial barriers, the Fisk Jubilee Singers took the music of sorrow and hope across the waters and around the country to raise money for their school. The Web site and 60-minute video provide interviews, a timeline, song lyrics, song sheets, and the history of this chorus.

Reader Response Opportunity

Graphic Organizer

1. Make a T-chart showing the similarities and differences between the information on the Web site and what is found in *A Band of Angels*.

2. Make a Bio Graph for one of the Jubilee Singers.

Open-Ended Response Opportunity

The singing of the Fisk Jubilee Singers made them welcome in places that excluded most African Americans. What do you think made the world embrace these songsters?

Paul Robeson (Video).
Executive Producer, Rex Barnett.
Atlanta, GA: History on Video, 1994.

This 36-minute black-and-white educational video details the controversial life of singer, actor, and political activist Paul Robeson. Robeson's powerful voice earned him acclaim, while his political beliefs and sympathies toward Russia launched him into an eight-year involuntary exile and subsequent years as an expatriate.

Reader Response Opportunity

1. Paul Robeson's career suffered as a result of his openly expressed political views. In your opinion, should public figures such as professional musicians, actors, and athletes publicly voice their opinions about politics and other controversial topics? Why?

2. Some people interpreted Robeson's views as unpatriotic. Is it unpatriotic to criticize policies of the United States? Support your opinion with examples.

3. Americans have protection for their freedom of speech. In your opinion, were Paul Robeson's rights violated? Explain.

Marian Anderson: The Story of the Voice That Broke Barriers.
WETA Washington Productions (Video).
Greater Washington Educational Telecommunications Association, 1991.
www.kulturvideo.com.

This video explores the life of an extraordinary talent and unveils a wellspring of virtue in a humble, strong, wise woman of color who lived and performed in Jim Crow America. 60 minutes.

Reader Response Opportunity

Open-Ended Response Opportunity

1. What do you most admire about Marian Anderson? Explain.

2. The Fisk Jubilee Singers and Marian Anderson acted as ambassadors for the United States as they traveled and performed in Europe. Is music effective in bringing people with differences together? How?

3. The Fisk Jubilee Singers and Marian Anderson performed before royalty in Europe and received gracious welcomes. Meanwhile, back in the United States they faced unfair treatment. How do you think they felt about this contradiction? Explain.

Additional music sites

http://www.infotoday.com.

http://www.freep.com/blackhistory/music/bhmusic6.htm.

http://www.2worldbook.com/features/aamusic/html/spirituals.

http://www.rhino.com/blackhistory/timeline.html.

http://www.africana.com/articles/tt_226.htm.

Reader Response Opportunity

1. Research African American music on one of these Web sites.

2. Create a collage, PowerPoint presentation, or other visual representation.

3. Prepare and present a musical performance.

WRITING PROMPTS

Elementary Writing Prompt

Music is very important for many reasons. Music often makes people feel better, and it is frequently part of main events.

```
Write about the importance of music in your life
```

Secondary Writing Prompt

From primitive drums to sophisticated synthesizers, throughout history music has played an important part in the lives of people of all cultures.

```
Write about the importance of music in culture.
```

Multilevel Writing Prompt

During the late 1990s, financial problems sometimes led states to reduce funding for music education in public schools.

```
Write about the importance of music education in public schools.
```

11
▼▼▼▼▼

Plenty Good Room:
Kinfolk and Kindred

A family is like a forest; each tree has its own place.
—Akan proverb

Plenty Good Room

Plenty good room, plenty good room,
Plenty good room in my Father's kingdom.
Plenty good room, plenty good room,
So choose your seat and sit down.

Plenty good room, plenty good room,
Plenty good room in my Father's kingdom.
Plenty good room, plenty good room,
So choose your seat and sit down.

HISTORICAL CONTEXT

"Plenty good room, plenty good room." Traditionally the African American home has always had room for one more, room at the table for the unexpected dinner guest, room in the home for the wayward child, room for the motherless nephew, room for the misunderstood teenager, room for aging and ailing Big Mama, room for one more. As with the Hebrew patriarch Abraham, family has enduring worth, countless stars brilliantly illuminating life's darkest skies.

African Americans inherited this strong sense of family from their African forebears. Rural African families make their living farming, fishing, and raising livestock. African families customarily venerate their elders, work together as a unit, and regard the addition of family members by marriage or birth as gain not burden. In these primarily patrilineal cultures "Who's your daddy?" matters and family extends beyond mother, father, and children to incorporate the entire clan of kin supporting one another.

This emphasis on family and the extended family or clan has typified African family life since the ancient civilizations fashioned the continent. Traditionally, females performed the household duties of child rearing, making the home environment clean and pleasant, and preparing the family meals. Family served as the sole source of socialization in the Nubian civilization. Nubi strongly discouraged divorce, leaving scarce opportunities for divorced women and requiring repayment of the bridewealth. In the West African Mali Empire, arranged marriages and polygamy figure in the scheme of family planning. Also, on the West African coast the Ashanti, a rare matrilineal culture, still assemble for special occasions. Families come together to mark special rites of passage: child naming, coming of age, marrying, and dying. Clans presided over by chiefs or elders congregate for festivals. The Ibos of Nigeria emphasize community life. Each Ibo village consists of multiple extended families governed by a council of elders. Continuity, community, and unity summarize the strengths of African families.

Like an unskilled, back alley abortionist, the Atlantic slave trade savagely ripped Africa's children from her womb. In West Africa's villages, grandmothers and mothers wept for their children, children waited in vain for their fathers' return, and husbands yearned for their wives. Abruptly separated from their home, these family-oriented abductees found themselves on hostile shores. From slave dungeon to slave ship to auction block to plantation, the Atlantic slave trade persisted in tearing at the fabric of the African family. Once purchased, the fate of the family lay in the slave owner's hands. If permitted to marry, men and women had no guarantee of "till death do we part." Giving birth to a child gave a mother no assurance of raising the child as her own or of living long enough to see her children's children grow in grace. Sold and dispatched like chattel, husbands and wives, mothers and children, sisters and brothers bid one another painful farewells. Debt or death of the master might lead the owner to sell a family member without warning. Slavery and racism systematically set about shredding the fabric of the African family in America, but from the remnants African American families materialized.

Scores of years after emancipation, the aftershocks of slavery and the tremors of racism continue to shake the African American family. Yet family remains a precious possession. Grandparents hold an honored position and play an active role in their grandchildren's lives. The roots of the African American family tree lie deep beneath the verdant grasslands and forests of the African continent. Encompassing the past, present, and future, the African American is "a heritage from the Lord" (Psalm 127:3), embracing not only bonds established by blood or law but also relationships conceived in the heart and born of the spirit.

MIND MIXER: FAMILY TREE

1. Create a family tree of the ideal family and extended family you would choose.
2. Use photographs, magazine pictures, or drawings on your family tree.
3. Share your family tree with a partner or in a small group of 2 to 4 students, and explain whom you placed on your family tree and why.

VOCABULARY

chamber	initiation	rubble
colossal	juncture	saltpans
crested	kindred	saturate
cycad	matrilineal	sequestered
dismantle	miscegenation	sentry
familial	mulatto	sorcerer
gorge	patrilineal	sundry
hallowed	plumage	titan
harem	polygamy	venerate
inaccessible	python	vigil
indigo	ricochet	wildebeest
inexplicable	rite	

FOLKLORE

Land of Legends
(Based on Vha Venda folklore)
▼▼▼▼▼

In the Land of Legends long after the Titan Khuswane walked in the Valley of Giants, Ndazi flew on wings of thunder and Nethathe the White Lion guarded the dense, dark secrets of the Sacred Forest and its yellowwoods, cycads, stinkwoods, ferns, and *nkoa*, the colossal mushrooms. Sundry feathered creatures—Guinea fowls, doves, cuckoos, hawks, falcons, vultures, and ostriches—painted the canvas of this African paradise in emerald, ivory, indigo, gray, ebony, gold, pink, and crimson. Harems of holy baboons stood guard atop the rocky hills warding off intruders. Herds of elephants tramped in giant footprints left thousands of years before by the long-necked dinosaur. Giraffes, blue wildebeests, antelopes, and zebras roamed freely on the savannahs and within the mystical forests. The hallowed white crocodile and broken-hearted Domba the Python sequestered themselves beneath the waters of Lake Fundudzi longing for fulfillment.

In this magical setting the ancient baobab tree welcomed Chief Dabanyika and the VhaVenda people to their Canaanland in the Njelele Valley. *"Dzata,"* a good place, Dabanyika and his people declared as they set their eyes on this promising land rich with trees of all kinds, exotic animals, iron, salt-pans, copper, ivory, and gold. The VhaVenda people settled into this diverse homeland of majestic waterfalls, rivers, hot springs, valleys, red sand dunes, and gorges. The golden age of Vendaland had begun.

Chief Dabanyika, leader of the VhaVenda, married a comely Venda maiden named *Lhosa* who gave birth to three sons. Dabanyika named his youngest son, Thohoyandau, head of the elephant. Thohoyandau adored Dabanyika and followed his path toward greatness. Likewise Dabanyika's soul exploded with pride for Thohoyandau who had the strength of an elephant. One day Dabanyika and his beloved son went hunting in the forbidden forest with Nguni, their dog. Following the scent of a wildebeest, Nguni raced ahead of his masters into a cave. The third born, Thohoyandau, ran to the mouth of the cave.

"*Vha khou ya ngafhi, Thohoyandau?* Where are you going, Thohoyandau?" asked Dabanyika.

"Father, Nguni must not go into the caves alone. He will get lost. I will go with Nguni. He is braver than he is wise," Thohoyandau answered.

"*Hai, Thoho.* No, Thoho. It is forbidden. I will enter and fetch Nguni. You wait here in case *gnu,* the wildebeest, runs out."

"*Ee,* Father. Yes, Father. *Mashudu.* Good luck," Thohoyandau bid his father.

"My arrow is sharp and ready. Gnu will not escape."

Dabanyika stooped to enter the cave, calling out to Nguni as he ventured further into its shadows. "*Nguni, Nguni, vha khou ita mini*? *Nguni, Nguni, vha khou ita mini?* Nguni, Nguni, what are you doing? Nguni, Nguni, what are you doing?" Dabanyika's calls ricocheted among the dark, damp chambers of the cave. The rocks replied. Waiting outside the cave entrance, Thohoyandau heard Nguni's bark and a noise that was like the thunderous rumbling of 100 ngoma drums. Nguni raced out of the cave just ahead of the collapse, but Dabanyika and the wildebeest did not come out.

Nguni whined and dug at the debris until his paws were bloody. Thohoyandau tunneled through the rocks, calling his father's name. Finally, Chief Dabanyika's voice cried out from beneath the rubble.

"*Khombo, Thohoyandau.* Danger, Thohoyandau. Even with the strength of *ndou,* the most powerful elephant, you cannot save me. Nguni has led me to my burial place. You must leave before the stones again begin to fall. Promise me you will unite our people and make a great nation of the Venda. *Nda ndou.* Good day, Elephant."

"*Hai,* Father, *hai!* No, Father, no! I will not leave you to die. Nguni and I will get you out."

"*Ee,* Little Elephant! Yes, Little Elephant. Go. Death like *Domba* the White Python wraps itself around me even now. Go."

"*Ndi a ni funa.* I love you, Father. *Kha vha sale.* Goodbye," Tohoyandau tearfully yet obediently bid his father farewell.

▼▼▼▼▼

In the wake of Chief Dabanyika's death, Thohoyandau fulfilled his father's last wish. The Venda nation led by Thohoyandau and all the chiefs who followed built great structures equal to the Zimbabwe ruins and introduced terrace farming to the region. The Venda left a legacy of fine gold artifacts, impressive ruins, terraced farms, and coffers full of legendary treasures: bewitched forests, mythical creatures, ancient relics, sacred sites, mysterious initiation rites, magical myths, and lasting legends.

In the eighth century at the juncture where South Africa meets Zimbabwe, Chief Dabanyika, or Dimbanyika, brought his people to settle in the Njelele Valley in the Soutpansberg Mountains region. His son Thohoyandau assumed power after the first chief's death. Vendaland lore features much that is mystical and inexplicable. Legend saturates the spirit world of Fundudzi Lake. Lovesick Domba walked into the waters and became the white python, god of fertility. The sacred white crocodile purportedly swam in this same lake that now hosts remnants of the crocodile family. Faithful as the sentries who defended the walls of Jerusalem in the day of Nehemiah, highly venerated baboons continue to keep vigil on the rocky hilltops of Lwamondo. Venda descendants continue to wrestle with *baloyi,* sorcerers and vampires, and *ngangas,* witch doctors. *Tshikovha,* the Medicine Man, holds court while the tireless traveler visits the Elephant Trunk baobab and the stone ruins and tombs at Thulamela and views colossal million-year-old footprints sculpted by Kokwane the Giant. A capital of the Venda nation stands as a witness to a loyal son, Thohoyandau, who had the strength and leadership of an elephant.

Reader Response Opportunity

Prewriting

Complete a Folklore Chart on "Land of Legends."

Open-Ended Response Opportunity

1. The Venda people believed they had arrived at their holy city, their promised land. Research the Aztec capital, Tenochtitlan, or the Israelite capital of Jerusalem, or the Israelite promised land, Canaan. Compare and contrast the establishment of either of these spiritual homes with that of Dzata/Vendaland.

2. VhaVenda superstition proposes that waving a hyena's tail will result in clear skies. List any superstitions you have heard or read. Explain and discuss any superstition you have heard of, in any culture. How/why do you think superstitions get started?

3. VhaVenda adolescent girls and boys undergo separate rites of passage to mark their coming of age. In what ways does American culture or any other ethnic culture celebrate a young person coming of age? Does your family have any special traditions to celebrate special occasions such as a sixteenth birthday, first communion, baptism, quinceñera, or a Bar Mitzvah? Explain.

TRADITIONAL SOUTHERN FOOD FARE

From Adam and Eve's garden snack of forbidden fruit to the Messiah's Last Supper with the chosen twelve, kinfolk and kindred have flavored familial bonds by breaking bread together. Today's sought-after soul food specialties that are featured at family reunions, Sunday suppers, holiday meals, and church fellowships first found their way into the bellies of enslaved men, women, and children in America's south from their self-appointed masters' tables. Unwanted pig parts and inexpensive, easily accessible greens and beans made tasty eating for forced laborers who worked the land for little reward. Cooks prepared a mess of cabbage, kale, collard greens, turnip greens, mustard greens, pinto beans, white beans, black-eyed peas, cowpeas, fatback, salt pork, neckbones, ham hocks, and pig's feet. In America's south, as in Africa, the womenfolk slowly simmered their peas, beans, or greens in a large pot, producing an unmistakable aroma to the soul food gourmet.

Reader Response Opportunity

1. Research southern recipes for greens, black-eyed peas, cowpeas, or beans. Select one recipe.
   - Give background information on the recipe.
   - List the ingredients and materials needed for one of the recipes.

- Make a Cycle Graph showing the steps to prepare the recipe.
- Write an explanatory composition about preparing your selection.

2. Research slave cooking. Discuss your findings.

3. Research South African recipes. Select one recipe.

   - Give background information on the recipe.
   - List the ingredients and materials needed.
   - Make a Cycle Graph showing the steps in preparing your choice.
   - Write a how-to composition about your recipe.

4. Research Abby Fisher, the first African American to publish her own recipes. Write a brief profile of her life or make a Cycle Graph showing the steps it took for her to get her recipes published.

5. Research *shambas*. How similar are *shambas* to antebellum North American plantations?

6. Research *umngqusho,* a South African dish and reportedly the favorite food of Nelson Mandela. Discuss the process of preparing *umngqusho*.

7. Research Nelson Mandela.

   - Make a Bio Graph of Nelson Mandela's life.
   - Write a character profile on Nelson Mandela.
   - Make a Venn diagram showing the similarities and differences between Nelson Mandela and Dr. Martin Luther King, Jr.
   - Compare the work of Nelson Mandela to Dr. Martin Luther King, Jr.

Suggested Research Sites

http://www.africaguide.com/cooking.htm.

http://www.congocookbook.com/c0202.html.

http://library.thinkquest.org/10320/Recipes.htm.

http://www.soulfoodcookbook.com/vegetables.html.

http://southernfood.about.com/library/weekly/aa082298.htm.

(Search words: *South African recipes, slave cooking, southern cooking, greens, beans, African American recipes, black-eyed peas, Mandela*)

PICTURE BOOK SELECTIONS

Family.
Isabell Monk. Illustrated by Janice Lee Porter.
Minneapolis, MN: Carolrhoda, 2001.

A family reunion brings together cousins, aunts, uncles, and other kinfolk and their distinct contributions to a potluck supper: homemade rolls, corn pudding, fresh greens, steamed corn on the cob, sliced red tomatoes, barbecue chicken, crab cakes, homemade lemonade, coconut cake, homemade ice cream, and dill pickles stuffed with peppermint sticks. Good food, good fun, good conversation, young folks and old folks. "Sharing food is a good way of sharing family."

Reader Response Opportunity

Prewriting

List favorite foods of your family.

Open-Ended Response Opportunity

1. What does the reader learn about this family from their reunion?
2. Does your family have reunions, get-togethers, or some other traditions? Explain.
3. How important is it for families to get together? Explain.
4. How important is food to family gatherings and family celebrations?

Grandmother and I.
Helen E. Buckley. Illustrated by Jan Ormerod.
New York: Lothrop, Lee, & Shepard, 1994.

Grandmother and I showcases the incomparable, inexplicable bond between grandma and grandchild. Mother's lap suffices for plaiting hair, daddy gives great pony rides on his lap, "Brothers and sisters let you ride on their backs," Grandpa's lap is a decent resting place for short respites, but only Grandma's lap feels "just right" all the time. Grandmother's lap swaddles, soothes, and shields. Grandma's lap, the hum of her voice, and the steady rhythm of the hardwood rocking chair shut out life's noises and minimize life's scary moments. Ms. Buckley also wrote *Grandfather and I* (1994) in which, Grandpa, never in a hurry, and the narrator take slow walks exploring nature's offerings until someone tells them to hurry.

Reader Response Opportunity

Prewriting

Make a T-chart contrasting the child's relationship with the other family members and with grandmother.

Open-Ended Response Opportunity

Describe a person or pet, real or imaginary, who gives you the safe feeling that grandmother's lap gives the narrator. Explain your choice.

When I Am Old with You.
Angela Johnson. Illustrated by David Soman.
New York: Orchard Books, 1990.

Coretta Scott King Honor Book.

A grandson expresses his heart longings of growing old with Granddaddy: sitting on the front porch at granddaddy's side in a big rocking chair, fishing at the old pond, eating out of a picnic basket and drinking cool water from a jug, playing cards all day until the lightning bugs come out, revisiting past memories, and journeying full circle back to the front porch, rocking side by side.

Reader Response Opportunity

Graphic Organizer/Prewriting

1. Make a cluster or web showing all the activities the boy wants to share with his Grand-daddy.

2. List all the activities you would like to share with a loved one if it were possible.

Open-Ended Response Opportunity

1. What do the wished-for activities tell you about the boy and about where he might live?

2. (Secondary/Post-Secondary) What paradox/contradiction is there in the title and in the whole premise of *When I Am Old with You*? Explain.

Quinnie Blue.
Dinah Johnson. Illustrated by James Ransome.
New York: Henry Holt, 2000.

An energetic, inquisitive young girl speculates about the grandmother whose name she bears. Did Grandma Quinnie Blue walk outside barefoot? Did Grandma Quinnie Blue bravely walk down the church aisle and testify in front of a waiting congregation? Whom on the family tree did Grandma Quinnie Blue resemble? Portrayed on a South Carolina canvas with a two-story porched house, sunflowers, bare feet, worms, wet grass, handclapping, and a tree swing, the young girl sings a "sassy womanchild song" with rhythmic ruminations.

Reader Response Opportunity

Prewriting

List all the questions the girl imagines asking her grandmother.

Open-Ended Response Opportunity

1. What poetic devices does the author use in *Quinnie Blue*? Explain.

2. How does the story make you feel?

3. Research your name. What does your name mean? How did you get your name? Do other family members have your name? How important are names?

4. Write a list of questions you would like to ask a favorite family member, godparent, or family friend about his/her childhood.

Grandpa's Face.
Eloise Greenfield. Illustrated by Floyd Cooper.
New York: Philomel Books, 1988.

An unfamiliar look on Grandpa's face stirs up "scared places" in Tamika's stomach. To ensure that the cold face will never be meant for her, Tamika tests the boundaries of Grandpa's love by misbehaving. "Time for a talk-walk," Grandpa declares. Their talk-walk to the park and back home reassures Tamika of her grandfather's unchanging love for her.

Reader Response Opportunity

Prewriting

Make a web showing everything Tamika loves about her grandpa.

Open-Ended Response Opportunity

1. Think of a person or pet you love. Make a web showing everything you love about that person or pet.
2. Write a poem or paragraph about your choice.

She Come Bringing Me That Little Baby Girl.
Eloise Greenfield. Illustrated by John Steptoe.
New York: HarperCollins, 1974.

Mama comes home from the hospital bringing "that little baby girl," and Kevin adamantly refuses to like her. Kevin does not want to be a brother. That baby girl is too small to throw a football, she has wrinkles, she cries too loud, and she is a girl. Then Mama puts that baby girl in his lap and enlists his help. Kevin slips into the role of protective, big brother as easily as butter slides on an ear of corn. This makes a great companion to another sibling rivalry book, *Julius, Baby of the World*, by Kevin Henkes, (1990). (*Objet trouve:* miniature football)

Reader Response Opportunity

Prewriting

Make a Cycle Graph or Ring Graph showing the progression of events from the moment Mama comes home with the baby girl.

Open-Ended Response Opportunity

1. What does Kevin not like about his baby sister?
2. Are Kevin's feelings when his sister first comes home typical? Explain.
3. How do Kevin's feelings change?
4. How do you think Kevin's life will change with a new sister?
5. Do you think Kevin will be a good big brother? Explain.

Paired-Text Reader Response Opportunity

Julius, Baby of the World and *She Come Bringing That Baby Girl.*

Prewriting

1. Make a T-chart showing the similarities between the two books.
2. Make a T-chart showing the advantages and disadvantages of having brothers and sisters.

Open-Ended Response Opportunity

1. (Elementary) How would you feel if you had a baby sister or brother? Why?
2. (Secondary) What do both books show us about sibling relationships? Explain.

Composition

Is it better to be an only child or to have siblings? Write an essay to convince a classmate of your opinion.

Back Home.
Gloria Jean Pinkney. Illustrated by Jerry Pinkney.
New York: Puffin Books, 1992.

Eight-year-old Ernestine rides the train to the ancestral home of her mother down South, back home to Lumberton, North Carolina. Her mother's old scrapbook, an old steamer trunk, an abandoned farmhouse, and the trio of Uncle June, Aunt Beula, and Cousin Jack make the Avery family farm feel like home to Ernestine. (*Objet trouve:* hard corn kernels, scrapbook page)

Reader Response Opportunity

Graphic Organizer

Make a cluster or timeline showing Ernestine's experiences during her visit back home.

Open-Ended Response Opportunity

1. Select an item from a family scrapbook. Interview a family member about the item and write about it.
2. Select an item you would place in your own scrapbook. Describe the item, and explain the item's significance and why you chose it.

Back Home Journey

Write about a visit to a place important to a parent or other elder relative. If you have never made such a visit, write about what you think you might see and experience based on what you have heard about it.

Hope.
Isabell Monk. Illustrated by Janice Lee Porter.
Minneapolis, MN: Carolrhoda Books, 1999.

Hope, a lovely biracial child, is the consummation of the faith of her mother's enslaved ancestors and the dreams of her father's European immigrant forebears. Family stories fill the weekends that Hope and Aunt Poogee spend together, stories of Grandpa Jack and Great-Grandma Nellie, stories of chickens flying in trees to escape the frying pan, and kitties and skunks and a bath in tomato juice. After hearing a troubling question about her heritage from Aunt Poogee's childhood friend, a story about Hope's parents settles Hope's uncertainties. (*Objet trouve:* red licorice)

Two Mrs. Gibsons.
Toyomi Igus. Illustrated by Daryl Wells.
San Franscisco: Children's Book Press, 1996.

Short, curly hair and long, straight black hair. A hearty laugh and a hidden laugh. Dainty pen strokes and joyful spirituals. Fireflies and paper cranes. A little girl compares her Japanese mother and her African American grandmother, two Mrs. Gibsons. (*Objet trouve:* chopsticks, origami)

Reader Response Opportunity

Graphic Organizers

1. Make a web showing Hope's characteristics.
2. Make a T-chart showing the differences between the two Mrs. Gibsons.
3. Make a Venn diagram showing the similarities and differences between the two books, *Hope* and *Two Mrs. Gibsons*.

Open-Ended Response Opportunity

(Secondary/Post-Secondary)

1. Define *miscegenation.*
2. Research miscegenation laws. On a T-chart list the pros and cons of being of mixed heritage, whether ethnic, cultural, or religious. Then write an essay about it.
3. Research the Thomas Jefferson–Sally Heming relationship. Do you believe Sally Heming's descendants should be welcomed at Jefferson family reunions? Write a persuasive essay supporting your opinion.

NOVEL SELECTIONS

Sister.
Eloise Greenfield. Illustrated by Moneta Barnett.
New York: HarperCollins, 1974.

New York Times Outstanding Book of the Year.

A widowed mother and her two teenaged daughters struggle to make sense of the world and their family: thirteen-year-old Doretha, defiant Alberta, and Mama. In her notebook, *My Doretha Book—Memories,* Doretha records her personal discoveries about herself and her kin as she day-dreams, reviews her family's good ole times, "sister good" times, and troubled times, learns about her African heritage in a basement apartment school, and attempts to make life right for her mother and her older sister.

Reader Response Opportunity

Graphic Organizer

1. Make a Bio Graph of Doretha's life.
2. Make a Venn diagram showing the similarities and differences between Alberta and Doretha.

Open-Ended Response Opportunity

1. Describe the relationship between Alberta and Doretha.
2. Describe the relationship between Doretha and Mama.
3. How do the two relationships differ?

Roll of Thunder, Hear My Cry.
Mildred D. Taylor.
New York: Dial Books for Young Readers, 1976.

Newbery Medal, 1977.

Mildred D. Taylor's novels chronicle the Logan family's troubles and triumphs as they fight to realize dreams long overdue. The 1930s and the Deep South add up to hard times for an African American family, but Papa reminds Cassie, the narrator, that the prized possessions of land and family promise security and success. Other Taylor novels not discussed in *Talking Drums* include *Song of the Trees* (1975), *Let the Circle Be Unbroken* (1981), *The Road to Memphis* (1990), *Mississippi Bridge* (1990), and *The Well* (1995).

Reader Response Opportunity

Graphic Organizer

Create a Ring Graph or a Cycle Graph of pivotal events in *Roll of Thunder, Hear My Cry.*

Open-Ended Response Opportunity

1. Give specific examples of how the Logans' lives might have been different if they were not African Americans.
2. Write 7 to 10 questions you would ask the author, Mildred D. Taylor, if you had a chance to interview her. Explain why you would choose these questions.

Toning the Sweep.
Angela Johnson.
New York: Scholastic Inc., 1993.

1994 Coretta Scott King Award; School Library Journal Best Book of 1993; Booklist Editor's Choice, 1993.

Toning the sweep, letting go, setting free. In South Carolina folklore this act of hitting a plow with a hammer sets souls free. Diagnosed with cancer, Grandmama Ola prepares to leave her life in the desert and move in with her daughter and granddaughter. In the shadow of the frightening changes that the cancer sets in motion, Grandmama Ola, Mama, and Emmie tone the sweep. Each in her own way rings away the past, sweeping away the sting of loss. The brilliance of love and abundant life shine throughout this story about letting go and moving on like the desert sun.

Reader Response Opportunity

1. The color yellow dominates the visual images in the book. List some of the sensory images from *Toning the Sweep.*
2. Which woman in *Toning the Sweep* is most interesting to you? Why? Describe the character.
3. Which character is most successful at letting go of the past? Explain.

NONFICTION SELECTIONS

Slaves in the Family.
Edward Ball.
New York: Farrar, Straus & Giroux, 1998.

Edward Ball makes an honest, penetrating disclosure of his family's relationship with slaves.

Roots: The Saga of an American Family.
Alex Haley.
New York: Doubleday, 1976.

Alex Haley's majestic saga of his family's history from the Slave Coast of Africa to slavery in America captivated the nation.

MULTIMEDIA

Texas Slave Families.
Ruthe Winegarten.
http://www.humanities-interactive.org/texas/rural/tx_slave_families.htm.
March–April, 1985.

Documenting the American South.
http://www.docsouth.unc.edu/neh/nehmain.html.
Academic Affairs Library, the University of North Carolina at Chapel Hill, 1998.

Born in Slavery: Slave Narratives from the Federal Writers' Project, 1936–1938.
http://memory.loc.gov/cgi~bin/ampage.

Slave Narratives.
Norman R. Yetman.
http://lcweb2.loc.gov/ammem/snhtml/snintor00.html.

Reader Response Opportunity

1. Browse the selected site. Write a profile on an interviewee.
2. What does the person's narrative reveal about him or her and life at the time.
3. Rewrite a portion of the narrative in standard American English.
4. Write 7 to 10 questions you would ask an ex-slave if you could.
   Why you would ask these particular questions?

Reader Response Opportunity

Graphic Organizer

Make a Venn diagram or t-chart comparing and contrasting the families in *Roots* and *Slaves in the Family*.

Open-Ended Response

How does slavery impact both families, the family of Alex Haley and the family of Edward Ball?

WRITING PROMPTS

Elementary Writing Prompt

Food is often a key ingredient of family celebrations and get-togethers.

Write about a favorite family food.

Secondary Writing Prompt

Edward Ball and Alex Haley spent countless hours researching their family histories.

Write about the importance of knowing your family history.

Multilevel Writing Prompt

Many people believe in marrying a person with a similar background, religious beliefs, and ethnicity. Others marry someone who has a different background from their own.

What qualities should a person consider in choosing a person to love or marry?

APPENDIX A
▼▼▼▼▼

NCTE/IRA Standards and Correlates

STANDARDS FOR THE ENGLISH LANGUAGE ARTS

The focus or key words of each standard are paraphrased below. To see the full texts of the standards, access the National Council of Teachers of English Web site at http://www.ncte.org/standards/standards.shtml.

1. Culturally diverse texts.
2. Many genres of literature.
3. Reading strategies.
4. Spoken, written, and visual language.
5. Writing process.
6. Generate, evaluate, and discuss.
7. Research.
8. Technology and information sources.
9. Diversity in language and culture.
10. Language skills for ESL and LEP.
11. Participation in literary community.
12. Speak, write, and create (NCTE, 2003).

NCTE/IRA CORRELATES IN *TALKING DRUMS*

Oral Tradition: Proverbs, Spirituals, and Folklore

Standards 1, 2, 3, 9, 10, and 12

Historical Context

Standards 1, 9, and 10

Mind Mixer

Standards 4, 6, 10, 11, and 12

Vocabulary

Standards 3 and 12

Food Fare

Standards 4, 5, 6, 7, 9, 10, and 12

Picture Book, Novel, and Nonfiction Text Selections

Standards 1, 2, 3, 6, 9, and 10

Multimedia

Standards 1, 6, 7, 8, and 10

Reader Response Opportunities

Standards 3, 4, 5, 6, 7, 10, 11, and 12

Writing Prompts

Standards 4, 5, 6, 8, 10, 11, and 12

APPENDIX B
▼▼▼▼▼

TAKS Objectives and Correlates

TAKS OBJECTIVES

Reading Grades 3–8

1. Culturally diverse texts.
2. Literary elements.
3. Analyze texts.
4. Higher-level thinking.

Writing Grades 4 and 7

1. Effective writing.
2. Language control.
3. Organization.
4. Sentences.
5. Word choice.
6. Proofreading.

English Languages Arts/Reading Grades 9 and Exit Level 10/11

1. Culturally diverse texts.
2. Literary elements and techniques.
3. Analyzing and evaluating.

English Language Arts Exit Level 10/11

4. Effective writing.
5. Mechanics and language control.
6. Proofreading.

Social Studies Grades 8, 10, and 11 Exit Level

1. Events and issues of U.S. history.
2. Geography.
3. Economic and social influences.
4. Politics.
5. Higher-level thinking (TEA).

TAKS CORRELATES IN *TALKING DRUMS*

Oral Tradition: Proverbs, Spirituals, and Folklore

TAKS Reading Objectives Grades 3–8: 1–4

TAKS Reading Objectives Grade 9: 1–3

TAKS English Language Arts Objectives Grades 10 and 11: 1–3

Historical Context

TAKS Social Studies Objectives Grades 8, 10, and 11: 1–4

Mind Mixer

TAKS Reading Objectives Grades 3–8: 4

TAKS Reading Objectives Grade 9: 3

TAKS English Language Arts Objectives Grades 10 and 11: 3

TAKS Social Studies Objectives Grades 8, 10, and 11: 5

Vocabulary

TAKS Reading Objectives Grades 3–8: 1

TAKS Reading Objectives Grade 9: 1

TAKS English Language Arts Objectives Grades 10 and 11: 1

Food Fare

TAKS Reading Objectives Grades 3–8: 3 and 4

TAKS Reading Objectives Grade 9: 1 and 3

TAKS English Language Arts Objectives Grades 10 and 11: 1 and 3

TAKS Social Studies Objectives Grades 10 and 11: 2, 3, and 5

Picture Books, Novels, and Nonfiction Selections

TAKS Reading Objectives Grades 3–8: 1–4

TAKS Reading Objectives Grade 9: 1–3

TAKS English Language Arts Objectives Grades 10 and 11: 1–3

TAKS Social Studies Objectives Grades 8, 10, and 11: 1–5

Multimedia

TAKS Reading Objectives Grades 3–8: 1, 2, and 4

TAKS Reading Objectives Grade 9: 1 and 3

TAKS English Language Arts Objectives Grades 10 and 11: 1 and 3

TAKS Social Studies Objectives Grades 8, 10, and 11: 1–5

Reader Response Opportunities

TAKS Reading Objectives Grades 3–8: 1–4

TAKS Reading Objectives Grade 9: 1–3

TAKS English Language Arts Objectives Grades 10 and 11: 1–3

TAKS Writing Objectives Grades 4 and 7: 2 and 3

TAKS English Language Arts Objectives Grades 10 and 11: 5

TAKS Social Studies Objectives Grades 8, 10, and 11: 5

Writing Prompts

TAKS Writing Objectives Grades 4 and 7: 1–6

TAKS English Language Arts Objectives Grades 10 and 11: 4–6

APPENDIX C

▼▼▼▼▼

Methali: Proverbs

Proverbs are the daughters of experience.

—African proverb

Africa

A tree cannot stand without roots.

Equality is difficult, but superiority is painful.

A sandstorm passes, the stars remain.

The wise are as rare as eagles soaring above the clouds.

Nothing is more dangerous than saving a hungry beast.

It is better to scratch for a living and be free than to be fed by a stranger's hand and land in the cooking pot.

People without knowledge of their own history are like trees without roots.

Akan

A family is like a forest; each tree has its own place.

Ashanti

Do not call the forest that shelters you a jungle.

Ethiopia

When spider webs unite, they can tie up a lion.

A loose tooth will not rest until it is pulled out.

Unless you call out, who will open the door?

Ghana

Wisdom is like a baobab tree; no one person can embrace it.

Hausa

Even the River Niger must flow around an island.

Igbo (Ibo)

Until lions have their own storytellers, tales of the hunt will always exalt the hunter.

Kenya

Sorrow is a precious treasure, shown only to friends.

Mayombe

Every stream has its source.

Nigeria

If the drum is not made, it is the fault of the master, but if it is not beaten, it is the fault of the drummers.

If we forget yesterday, how shall we remember tomorrow?

The man who remembers others remembers also his creator.

Zimbabwe

Long ago did not live long ago.

APPENDIX D
▼▼▼▼▼

Languages of Africa Glossary

Estimates for the number of indigenous African languages and dialects written and spoken by the continent's native inhabitants vary from 500 to 800 to thousands. In my research, I've found that the number of African languages in Ghana alone fluctuates from forty to one hundred. Additionally, some black Africans speak Arabic and several Indo-European languages, including Afrikaans, English, Dutch, and French. Included in this glossary are Bantu, Gullah, French, and Spanish words used in *Talking Drums*.

LANGUAGES OF AFRICA

Bantu: Any language of indigenous African origin.

Gullah: A hybrid blend of English and thousands of West African words that evolved among the Sea Island African Americans of the Carolinas and Georgia.

Ibo: A Kwa language of the Ibo people of Nigeria, Central Africa; a musical and rhythmic language, contingent on idioms and proverbs.

Kiswahili (Swahili Language): Language of the Wiswahili (Swahili) culture of East and Central Africa; official language in Kenya, Tanzania, and Uganda, and possibly the most widely used and known African language. Kanga writings and proverbs are part of Kiswahili oral tradition.

Luganda/Ganda: The most widely used Niger-Congo language; the native language of the Baganda people of Uganda.

Mandinka/Manding: Language of the former great Mali Empire; a Mande group language; language of nine nations with over ten million people; a tribal, oral tradition language.

Tshivenda/Venda: Language spoken by more than 800,000 Venda people in South Africa.

Twi/Akan: Most important language of Ghana; a Niger-Congo family language.

Yoruba: The second-largest language group in Africa; major Nigerian language spoken by twenty to thirty million inhabitants; a Kwa language of the Yoruba people of Nigeria and Bénin.

LANGUAGES OF AFRICA GLOSSARY

Each entry includes the meaning as used in the text and the language origin

Afua: Friday's female child. (Twi)

akadinda/amadinda: twelve-key log xylophone. (Bantu)

amistad: friendship. (Spanish)

Amma: Saturday's female child. (Twi)

arusi: wedding. (Kiswahili)

asante: thank you. (Kiswahili)

Asante Hene/Asantehene: Asante king, ruler of the Ashanti. (Akan)

au: with. (French)

baba: father. (Kiswahili)

Baganda: people of Buganda, largest ethnic group of Uganda. (Luganda)

baloyi: sorcerer, vampire. (Tshivenda)

Bantu: of indigenous African origin. (Bantu)

bitangole: the king's men. (Luganda)

bon appetite: good appetite. (French)

buka: lightning. (Luganda)

centimes: cent. (French)

cinq: five. (French)

Cote D'Ivoire: Ivory Coast. (French)

crevette: shrimp. (French)

cuisine: cooking. (French)

djeli/jeli: (ja-lee) royal historian and keeper of culture, storyteller, master drummer/musician. (Manding)

domba: python. (Tshivenda)

dzata: a good place. (Tshivenda)

ee: yes. (Tshivenda)

fromage: cheese. (French)

fufu: African staple of bananas, yams, rice. (Bantu)

Ganda: shortened form of Baganda; people of Buganda. (Luganda)

ggulu: sky. (Luganda)

glacé: sugared or candied. (French)

goober: peanut, groundnut. (Gullah)

gnu: wildebeest. (Tshivenda)

griot: (gree *oh*) Mande keeper of oral tradition and culture, storyteller. (French)

gumbo: okra; thick stew/soup with okra. (Bantu, Gullah)

habari: greeting between peers. (Kiswahili)

hai: no. (Tshivenda)

hujambo: Are you okay? familiar. (Kiswahili)

jambo: hello. (Kiswahili)

kabaka: king. (Luganda)

kabaka yekka: the king only. (Luganda)

kanzu: traditional long, cotton gown. (Luganda)

karibu: welcome. (Kiswahili)

kente: symbolic cloth with woven design, originally worn by Ashanti royalty, from the Ashanti kenten—basket. (Twi)

kha vha sale: good-bye. (Tshivenda)

khombo: danger. (Tshivenda)

ki: thing. (Luganda)

kiboko: hippopotamus. (Kiswahili)

kifaru: rhinoceros. (Kiswahili)

kima: monkey. (Kiswahili)

kiweewa: first-born son of the king. (Luganda)

kiwanuka: lightning. (Luganda)

Kofi: Friday's male child. (Twi)

kora: twenty-one-stringed harp made of a gourd covered with cowhide, used by *djeli*. (Manding)

Kwame: Saturday's male child. (Twi)

lakiko: crown's council, parliament. (Luganda)

mama: mother. (Kiswahili)

marahabaa: "I acknowledge your respect." (Kiswahili)

mashudu: good luck! (Tshivenda)

mbuzi: goat. (Kiswahili)

nana: grandfather, elder. (Kiswahili)

nda ndou: good day! (Tshivenda)

ndi a ni funa: I love you. (Tshivenda)

ndizi: banana. (Kiswahili)

ndovu: elephant. (Kiswahili)

nganga: witch doctor. (Tshivenda)

ng'ombe: cow. (Kiswahili)

ngoma: grand celebration, party, music. (Kiswahili)

nguni: dog. (Tshivenda)

nkoa: giant mushroom. (Tshivenda)

ntu: being. (Luganda)

oba: chief, leader. (Yoruba)

objet trouve: treasured object. (French)

Oduduwa: Ancestor of all. (Yoruba)

Oluyo Olulangira: Royal Clan. (Luganda)

omuhiire: good fortune. (Luganda)

omutuba: bark cloth tree. (Luganda)

orisha/orisa: deity, a demigod. (Yoruba)

poulet: chicken (French)

rafiki: friend. (Kiswahili)

Ruhanga: Creator. (Luganda)

Sengalaise: Sengalese, of Senegal (French)

shamba: African-style plantation. (Tshivenda)

Shikamoo: "I touch your feet." I respect you. Greeting from a younger to an older person. (Kiswahili)

Sijambo: I'm fine. (Familiar; Kiswahili)

simba: lion. (Kiswahili)

sungura: hare. (Swahili)

tembo: elephant. (Kiswahili)

thohoyandou: head of the elephant. (Tshivenda)

thulamela: physical position of respect. (Tshivenda)

tshikova: medicine man. (Tshivenda)

Tshivenda: language of the Venda people. (Tshivenda)

Vha khou ita mini?: Where are you going? (Tshivenda)

walumbe: death. (Luganda)

zeze: stringed instrument; great grandfather of banjo and guitar. (Swahili)

APPENDIX E

▼▼▼▼▼

Folklore Charts

ELEMENTARY FOLKLORE CHART

Title:

Who are the people or animals in the story?

Where does the story happen?

What happens in the story?

What problems do the people or animals have?

What happens at the end?

What other story is this one like? Why?

SECONDARY FOLKLORE CHART

Title:

Origin (country, culture):

Type of Folklore (myth, fable, folktale, legend, fairy tale):

Setting (time, place, environment):

Main characters:

Plot (cycle of events):

Conflict (problem):

Resolution (How is the conflict solved or resolved?):

Theme/Moral (main idea/lesson learned):

Similar Stories (List any similar fairy tales, fables, myths):

Explain the similarity:

APPENDIX F

▼▼▼▼▼

Rubrics

A rubric allows both the teacher and the student to know the expectations for an assignment. Students can prepare their writing assignments using the rubric for their guidelines. Teachers can holistically assess student work quickly and fairly using the rubric as the standard of measurement. With each rubric keep in mind the age, grade, and ability level of each student. Tailor the rubric to fit you and your students.

GRAPHIC ORGANIZER/PREWRITING STRATEGY RUBRIC

Outstanding—3

Exceeds expectations.

Shows creativity.

Acceptable—2

Follows directions.

Shows effort.

Has required number of entries or ideas.

Borderline—1

Has less than required ideas or entries.

Appears messy.

Shows lack of effort or thought.

Unsatisfactory—0

Does not address the topic.

Does not follow directions.

Was not submitted.

OPEN-ENDED SHORT ANSWER RUBRIC

Outstanding—3

Fully and reasonably addresses the question.

Supports answer with many specific, relevant details, quotes, etc. from the text.

Shows higher level thinking skills.

Acceptable—2

Answers major parts of the question.

Gives some support from the text.

Shows comprehension of the text.

Borderline—1

Attempts to answer the question in a general way.

Answers incorrectly or cites incorrect, irrelevant details from text.

Fails to support answer with evidence from the text.

Unsatisfactory—0

Does not answer the question asked.

Incorrectly answers the question.

Gives no response.

ELEMENTARY WRITING PROMPT RUBRIC

The writing . . .

Outstanding—4

Skillfully and creatively addresses the prompt.

Is well planned and well written.

Develops ideas with many details, quotations, examples, comparisons, figurative language, excellent word choices, etc.

Reflects higher-level thinking.

Is one of a kind.

Successful—3

Sufficiently addresses the prompt.

Is easy to follow and understand.

Develops ideas with some specific, relevant details, examples, quotes, etc.

Appropriately uses grade-level vocabulary.

Shows thoughtfulness.

Acceptable—2

Follows the directions.

Is loosely organized.

Briefly explains or supports ideas.

Uses some grade-level vocabulary.

Has many minor errors.

Unsatisfactory—1

Is too short.

Needs more details and examples.

Needs an introduction, support, or conclusion.

Has below grade-level vocabulary.

Is difficult to read and understand.

0

Does not follow the directions.

Is too sloppy to score.

SECONDARY/POST-SECONDARY WRITING PROMPT RUBRIC

Outstanding—4

Expertly addresses the prompt.

Is well organized.

Supports ideas with a wealth of relevant, in-depth, and creative elaboration.

Uses unique figurative language, vivid images, and advanced vocabulary.

Is well written with no or almost no errors.

Acceptable—3

Effectively addresses the prompt.

Is well organized.

Supports ideas with above-average, relevant elaboration.

Uses above-average vocabulary and descriptions.

Has no major errors and few minor errors.

Satisfactory—2

Addresses the prompt.

Is loosely organized.

Generically extends ideas with minimal or zero elaboration.

Uses average vocabulary.

Has some major and minor errors that distract from the writing.

Borderline—1

Vaguely addresses the prompt.

Lacks organization.

Is skeletal.

Uses slang, informal language, or inappropriate vocabulary.

Has frequent major and minor errors.

Unsatisfactory—0

The composition does not address the prompt.

Is too brief to evaluate.

Shows no control of the English language.

RESEARCH PROJECT/MULTIMEDIA PRESENTATION RUBRIC

The project/research . . .

Outstanding—4

Shows evidence of extensive effort and in-depth research.

Has unique, creative, and relevant visuals.

Is well presented, neat, and error free.

Has a maximum number of appropriately documented diverse sources.

Successful—3

Shows evidence of above-average effort and research.

Has relevant, interesting, above-average visuals.

Is well presented and neat with few minor errors.

Has appropriate documentation for a variety of sources.

Acceptable—2

Shows evidence of effort and surface level research.

Has acceptable, relevant visuals.

Is satisfactorily presented with minor errors.

Has the required number of correctly documented sources.

Borderline—1

Shows little evidence of effort or sufficient research.

Has messy, generic, or irrelevant visuals.

Has major or multiple errors.

Has insufficient documentation of sources.

Unsatisfactory—0

Shows no evidence of effort or research.

Lacks visual representation or has an incomplete or incorrect visual.

Has numerous errors or no text with the visual.

Has no documentation of sources.

Bibliography

Abdullah, Kassim. *About Kiswahili*. Retrieved March 24, 2003, from the Kiswahili Home Page. http://user.cs.tu-berlin.de/~frareg/swahili.html.

Adams, Cecil. *Are There Really Such Things as "Talking Drums"?* Retrieved March 13, 2003, from The Straight Dope. http://www.straightdope.com/classics/a5_158.html.

African American Odyssey. Retrieved April 24, 2003, from The Library of Congress Learning Page. http://memory.loc.gov/learn/collections/book/a.html.

African Americans. Retrieved January 7, 2003, from Oklahoma-at-a-Glance. http://www. okcareertech.org/ipr/ataglanc.htm.

African Christianity: A History of the Christian Church in Africa. Retrieved February 15, 2003, from African Christianity.http://www.bethel.edu/~letnie/AfricanChristianity. html.

African Cooking and Recipes. Retrieved April 22, 2003, from The Africa Guide. http://www.africaguide.com/cooking.htm.

African Folk Tales—Background Information. Retrieved June 10, 2003, from Teacher Vision.com. http://webcenter.netscape.teachervision.com/.

African Proverbs, Sayings, and Stories. Retrieved May 17, 2002, from Proverb Resources. http://cogweb.ucla.edu/Discourse/Proverbs.

Africans in America. Retrieved February 6, 2003, from PBS. http://www.pbs.org/wgbh/ aiapart1/1p263.html.

Agatucci, Cora. *African Slave Trade & European Imperialism*. Retrieved February 6, 2003, from African Timelines Part III. http://www.cocc.edu/cagatucci/classes/ hum211/.

Agatucci, Cora. *African Storytelling: Oral Traditions*. Retrieved February 6, 2003, from African Storytelling. http://www.cocc.edu/cagatucci/classes/hum211/afrstory.htm.

Ali, Hassan O. *A Brief History of the Swahili Language*. Retrieved January 16, 2003, from Hassan Ali's Home Page. http://www.glcom.com/hassan/index.html.

American Library Association. *ALSC: The John Newbery Medal*. Retrieved March 12, 2003, from the Association for Library Service to Children. http://www.ala.org.alsc/ nmedal.html.

American Library Association. *ALSC: The Randolph Caldecott Medal*. Retrieved March 12, 2003, from the Association for Library Service to Children. http://www.ala.org/ alsc/cmedal.html.

Appiah, Peggy. Illustrations by Peggy Wilson. *Ananse the Spider: Tales from an Ashanti Village.* New York: Pantheon Books, 1966.

Ayo, Yvonne. *Africa.* Photographs by Ray Moller and Geoff Dann. New York: Alfred A. Knopf, 1995.

Bailey, Cornelia. *I Am Sapelo.* Retrieved May 28, 2002, from Golden Isles Navigator. http://www.gacoast.com/navigator/iamsapelo.htm.

Benders-Hyde, Elisabeth. *Baobab.* Retrieved April 9, 2003, from Blue Planet Biomes. http://www.blueplanetbiomes.org/baobab.htm.

Black History Month. Retrieved May 28, 2002, from *Detroit Free Press.* http://www. freep.com/blackhistory/music/bhmusic6.htm.

Blauer, E. Hagale and Jason Lauré. *Ghana: Enchantment of the World.* New York: Children's Press, 1999.

Brecher, Jeremy. *The Amistad Incident.* Retrieved September 16, 2003, from Amistad Mystic Seaport. http://amistad.mysticseaport.org/timeline/amistad.html.

Bureau of Refugees, Freedmen and Abandoned Lands. Retrieved May 1, 2002, from Freedmen's Bureau Online. http://freedmensbureau.com/.

Calkins, Lucy. *The Art of Teaching Reading.* New York: Addison-Wesley Educational Publishers, 2001.

Carroll, Joyce Armstrong and Edward Wilson. *Acts of Teaching: How to Teach Writing.* Englewood, CO: Teacher Ideas Press, 1993.

Chronology of Emancipation during the Civil War. Retrieved May 1, 2002, from Freedmen and Southern Society Project. http://www.inform.umd.edu/ARHU/Depts/ History/Freedman/chronol.htm.

The Civil Rights Act of 1866. Retrieved April 25, 2002, from Afro-American Almanac. http://www.toptags.com/aama/docs/crts1866.htm.

Conway, Cecilia. *African Banjo Echoes in Appalachia: A Study of Folk Traditions.* Knoxville, TN: University of Tennessee Press, 1995.

Coretta Scott King Award. Retrieved March 12, 2003, from American Library Association. http://www.ala.org/srrt/csking/winners.html.

Cox, Clinton. *Undying Glory: The Story of the Massachusetts 54th Regiment.* New York: Scholastic Inc., 1991.

Cozzens, Lisa. *The Civil Rights Movement 1955–1965.* Retrieved April 19, 2003, from African American History. http://www.watson.org/~lisa/blackhistory/civilrights- 55-65/.

Creative Proverbs. Retrieved June 13, 2002, from Creative Proverbs from Around the World. http://creativeproverbs.com.

Curtis, Ken, Ed. *Slave Songs Transcend Sorrow. Slaves Sing Spirituals: "Let My People Go."* Retrieved November 18, 2003, from Gospelcom.net. http://www. gospelcom.net/chi/GLIMPSEF/ Glimpses/glmps089/shtml.

Dangoor, Naim. *African Tribe Presses for Recognition as Jews.* Retrieved July 18, 2003, from *The Scribe.* http://www.dangoor.com/72page25.html.

The Depression, the New Deal, and World War II. Retrieved April 25, 2002, from African American Odyssey, Library of Congress. http://memory.loc.gov/ammem/aaohtml/exhibit/aopart8.html.

DNA Holds Clues to African Origins of Many Americans. Retrieved November 14, 2002, from *The Black World Today* © 1996–2001. http://www.tbwt.com/news/.

Dobler, Lavenia and William Brown. *Great Rulers of the African Past.* New York: Doubleday, 1965.

Du Bois, W. E. B. "The Freedmen's Bureau." Retrieved May 1, 2002, from *The Atlantic Online.* http://www.theatlantic.com/issues/01mar/dubois.htm.

EnterUganda. Retrieved January 23, 2003, from Enter Uganda. http://www.enteruganda.com/about/history.php.

Estell, Kenneth. *African America: Celebrating 400 Years of Achievement.* Detroit: Visible Ink Press, 1994.

Exploring Amistad at Mystic Seaport. Retrieved June 10, 2002, from Amistad Mystic Seaport. http://amistad.mysticseaport.org.html.

Finnen, Wanda Cobb. "Walk Together, Children." *R & E Journal* 7. (Fall/Winter 1999/2001): 52–54.

Finnen, Wanda. "The East Side of the Garden." *R & E Journal* 8. (Fall/Winter 2000/2001): 54–55.

Finnen, Wanda. "Grains of Sand." *R & E Journal* 14. (Fall/Winter 2002/2003): 73–75.

Flonta, Teodor. *African Proverbs.* Retrieved May 17, 2002, from African Proverbs. http://cogweb.ucla.edu/Discourse/Proverbs/African.html.

Folk Tales. Retrieved June 10, 2002, from Afro-American Almanac. http://www.toptags.com/aama/tales/tales.htm.

Freedmen's Bureau. Retrieved May 1, 2002, from The Valley of the Shadow. http://www.iath.virginia.edu/vshadow2/HIUS403/freedmen/overview.html.

Freeman, Naquinda and Nakia Eas. *African Proverbs.* Retrieved March 10, 2003, from African Proverbs. http://www.philsch.k12.pa.us/schools/westphila/proverb2.html.

From Indentured Servitude to Racial Slavery. Retrieved February 6, 2003, from Africans in America. http://www.pbs.org/wgbh/aia/part1/1narr3.html.

Geblin, James. *Yoruba People.* Retrieved March 25, 2003, from Art & Life in Africa Online. http://www.uiowa.edu/~africart/toc/people/Yoruba.html.

Gibbon, Ed. *Congo Cookbook.* Retrieved April 9, 2003, from *Congo Cookbook.* http://www.congocookbook.com/c0202.html.

Hamilton, William. *54th Mass. Volunteer Infantry, Co I.* Retrieved April 15, 2002, from War@Charleston. http://www.awod.com/gallery/probono/cwchas/54ma.html.

Healey, Joe Rev. *African Proverbs, Sayings, and Stories.* Retrieved May 17, 2002, from African Proverbs, Sayings, and Stories. http://www.afriprov.org/resources/stories.

Gardner, Joseph L, ed. *Atlas of the Bible.* Pleasantville, NY: Reader's Digest Association, 1981.

Gates, Henry Louis. *Wonders of the African World.* New York: Alfred A. Knopf, 1999.

GhanaData. Retrieved November 14, 2002, from GhanaData.com. http://www.ghanadata. com/.

Great Kings of Africa. Retrieved June 10, 2003, from Great Kings of Africa. http:// home1.gte.net/ericnj/great_kings_of_Africa.htm.

Green, Lila. *The World Folktale Library: Tales from Africa.* Morristown, NJ: Silver Burdett, 1979.

The Harper's Ferry Insurrection. Retrieved April 25, 2002, from Afro-American Almanac. http://www.toptags.com/aama/events/hferry.htm.

Harrison, Algea. *The Importance of Including Grandparents in Services for African American Families.* Retrieved February 27, 2003, from the National Parent Information Network Virtual Library. http://npin.org/library/2001/n00599/n00599. html.

Heidelberg, Kenneth A. *Robert Gould Shaw and the 54th Regiment Memorial.* Retrieved May 1, 2002, from Boston African-American National Historic Site. http://www.nps.gov/boaf/ site1.htm.

Higginson, Thomas Wentworth. *Negro Spirituals.* Retrieved November 18, 2002, from University of Virginia Library. http://etext.lib.virginia.edu/.

The History of Juneteenth. Retrieved April 25, 2002, from Afro-American Almanac. http://www.toptags.com/aama/events/jtenth.htm.

History Official Site of Negro Spirituals. Retrieved November 22, 2002, from Negro Spirituals. http://www.negrospirituals.com/.

Horton, Hal. *Yoruba Religion and Myth.* Retrieved August 6, 2002, from African Literature in English in the Postcolonial. http://65.107.211.206/post/nigeria/yorubarel.html.

How Kintu Was Tested. Retrieved January 23, 2003, from Tales from Peoples of Sub-Saharan Africa. http://herkos.artsfac.csuohio.edu/tales/black_African/How_ Kintu_ Was_Tested.html.

Hyerle, David. *Visual Tools for Constructing Knowledge.* Alexandria, VA: ASCD, 1996.

The Internet Living Swahili Dictionary. Retrieved March 24, 2003, from The Kamusi Project. http://www.yale.edu/swahili/.

In the Field, Savannah, GA, January 16th, 1865. Retrieved April 25, 2002, from Afro-American Almanac. http://www.toptags.com/aama/docs/sforder15.htm.

Is Singleton's Movie a Scandal or a Black Schindler's List? Retrieved January 14, 2003, from *The Seminole Tribune.* http://www.seminoletribe.com/tribune/97/mar/rose wood.shtml.

Jane Addams Children's Book Award: Winners and Honor Books. Retrieved March 12, 2003, from Cooperative Children's Book Site. http://www.soemadison.wisc.edu/ccbc/addams/list.htm.

Jones, Anita R. *African Musical Instruments and Their Representation in African Art and Life.* Retrieved January 24, 2003, from African Musical Instruments: Representing Art and Life. http://cti.itc.virginia.edu/~arj4gshell5.html.

Jones, Maxine. *The Rosewood Report.* Retrieved July 15, 2002, from Rosewood. http://www.freenet.scri.fsu.edu/doc/rosewood.txt.

Keim, Karen. *Folktales: Ananse the Spider Trickster.* Retrieved January 16, 2003, from GhanaWeb. http://www.leheigh.edu/~tqr0/ghanaweb/folktales.html.

Kente. Retrieved June 5, 2002, from Republic of Ghana. http://www.ghana.com/republic/kente.

Keveren, Phillip. *African-American Spirituals.* Milwaukee, WI: Hal Leonard Corporation, 2000.

Khan, Iram and James Horner. *Africa—Where Stories Come From.* Retrieved January 16, 2003, from CanTeach. http://www.canteach.ca/elementary/africa2.html.

King James Bible (KJV). Chicago, IL: Good Counsel Publishers, 1965.

Knappert, Jan. *Kings, Gods, & Spirits from African Mythology.* New York: Peter Bedrick, 1986.

Lovelace, Alice. *The Tulsa Riot of 1921.* Retrieved January 7, 2002, from *In Motion* magazine. http://www.inmotionmagazine.com/tulsa19.html.

Maffly-Kipp, Laurie. *African-American Religion in the Nineteenth Century.* Retrieved September 17, 2003, from Divining America: Religion and the National Cultural. http://www.nhc.rtp.nc.us.8080/tserve/divam.html.

Mason-Middleton, Cheryl J. *Black Studies Library—Empathos National Library.* Retrieved July 26, 2002, from the empAΘos Nation Library. http://www.geocities.com/cjmasonm/Africa/africa.html.

Mathis, Kane. *Helpful African Proverbs.* Retrieved May 17, 2002, from Kane Proverbs. http://www.kairarecords.com/kane/proverbs.htm.

Matthews, Colleen. *Folk Tales.* Retrieved May 13, 2002, from Central Oregon Community College. http://www.cocc.edu/hum299/colleen/african/.

McKissack, Patrick and Fredrick McKissack. *The Royal Kingdoms of Ghana, Mali, and Songhay: Life in Medieval Africa.* New York: Henry Holt, 1994.

Methali Za Kiswahili—Swahili Proverbs. Retrieved March 9, 2003, from Mwambao. http://www.mwambao.com/methali.htm.

Metras, Mike. *The Baobab Tree.* Retrieved April 9, 2003, from Works and Words. http://www.worksandwords.com/etravels/baobab.htm.

Mildred D. Taylor. Retrieved February 22, 2003, from The Mississippi Writers Page. http://www.olemiss.edu/mwp/dir/taylor_mildred/.

Moonlit Road—Ibo Landing: Sea Island Slavery. Retrieved August 4, 2002, from Moonlit Road. http://www/mr.com/ibo/ibo_cbg002.html.

Motherland Nigeria: Proverbs. Retrieved March 8, 2002, from Motherland Nigeria. http://www.motherlandnigeria.com/proverbs.html.

Mukasa, Ssemakula E. *The Founding of Buganda*. Retrieved January 23, 2003, from Buganda Home Page. http://www.buganda.com/kintu.htm.

NCTE/IRA Standards for the English Language Arts. Retrieved September 15, 2003, from NCTE and IRA. http://www.ncte.org/standards/standards/shtml.

Newman, Richard. *Spirituals, African American*. Retrieved April 16, 2003, from African.com. http://www.african.com/articles/tt_266.htm.

New National Baptist Hymnal. National Baptist Publishing Board. Nashville, TN: Triad Publications, 1977.

Olivier, Jako. *Tshivenda: Venda*. Retrieved February 24, 2003, from South African Languages. http://www.cyberserv.co.za/users/~jako/lang/venda.htm.

On the Front Lines with the Little Rock 9. Retrieved December 14, 2002, from The American Experience. http://www.pbs.org/wgbh/amex/kids/civilrights/features_school.html.

Opoku, Kofi Asare. *African Proverbs*. Retrieved May 17, 2003, from Princeton Online. http://www.princetonol.com/groups/iad/lessons/middle/af-prov.ht.

Origin of "Jim Crow." Retrieved April 25, 2002, from Afro-American Almanac. http://www.toptags.com/aama/docs/jcrow.htm.

Otto of Freising: The Legend of Prester John. Retrieved July 18, 2003, from *Medieval Sourcebook*. http://www.fordham.edu/halsall/source/otto-prester.html.

Oxley, Lynette. *Louis Trichart, Thoyandou: A Cultural Land of Myths and Legends*. Retrieved June 20, 2003, from Adventure Articles. http://www.adventures.co.za/ven_art.htm.

Painted Voices. Retrieved March 12, 2003, from *The Black Collegian* Online. http://www.black-collegian.com/african/painted-voices/.shtml.

Papa, Maggie, Amy Gerber, and Abeer Mohamed. *African American Culture through Oral Tradition*. Retrieved May 13, 2002, from The George Washington University. http://www.gwu.edu/~e73afram/ag-am-mp.html.

Pazant, Bradford. *The Gullah Culture*. Retrieved August 4, 2003, from The Gullah Culture. http://www.ncat.edu/~pazantb/.

The People of Ghana: Dignified and Diverse. Retrieved March 25, 2003, from Global Volunteers. http://www.globalvolunteers.org/1main/Ghana/ghanapeople.htm.

Prester John-Geography. Retrieved July 18, 2002, from What You Need to Know about Geography. http://geography.about.com/library/weekly/aa081098.htm.

Prime Origins. Retrieved February 24, 2003, from Prime Origins. http://www.primeorigins.co.za.

Proverbs. Retrieved March 10, 2003, from SwahiliOnline. http://www.swahilionline.-com/language/ proverbs/provrbs.htm.

The Pulitzer Prize. Retrieved March 12, 2003, from Literature Awards. http://www. literature-awards.com/pulitzer_prize.htm.

Raboteau, Albert J. *African-American Religion.* New York: Oxford University Press, 1999.

Railton, Stephen. *Hymns & Spirituals.* Retrieved November 18, 2003, from *Uncle Tom's Cabin* & American Culture. http://Jefferson.village.Virginia.edu/utc/christn/ chsohp.html.

Rattray, Diana. *Southern Food History.* Retrieved November 1, 2002, from Southern U.S. Cuisine. http://southernfood.about.com/library/weekly/aa082298.htm.

Recer, Paul. *Fossil Suggests Diverse Migration.* Retrieved July 26, 2003, from *AP Science Writer.* http://iranscope.ghandchi.com/Anthology/SciTechMisc/migration. htm.

Remembering Rosewood. Retrieved January 14, 2003, from Displays for Schools. http://www.displaysforschools.com/rosewood.html.

The Rosewood Report History. Retrieved January 9, 2003, from The Rosewood Report History. http://members.aol.com/klove01/rosehist.htm.

Rotondo-McCord, J. *Origins and Neighbors.* Retrieved March 25, 2003, from Sacred and Secular in the African Americas. http://webusers.xula.edu/jrotondo/Kingdoms/ Mali/MaliOrigins01.htm.

Sandler, Bea. *The African Cookbook.* Retrieved April 22, 2003, from African Studies Center—University of Pennsylvania. http://www.sas.upenn.edu/African_Studies/ Cookbook/about_cb_wh.html.

Schlosser, Jim. *Launch of a Civil Rights Movement.* Retrieved April 19, 2003, from Greensboro Sit-Ins. http://www.sitins.com/.

School Desegregation and Equal Educational Opportunity. Retrieved December 14, 2002, from Civil Rights Org. http://www.civilrights.org/research_center/civilrights101/ desegregation.html.

Simkin, John. *Slave Families.* Retrieved February 19, 2003, from Spartacus Educational. http://www.spartacus.schoolnet.co.uk/USASseparation.htm.

Some Traditions and Stories of the Ganda. Retrieved January 23, 2003, from A Treasury of African Folktale. http://www.marcusgarvey.com/tales066.htm.

The Story of Africa: West African Kingdoms. Retrieved May 21, 2002, from World Service. http://www.bbc.co.uk/worldservice/africa/features/storyofafrica/4chapter44. shtml.

Sunday School Publishing Board. *Gospel Pearls.* Washington, DC: National Baptist Convention, USA, 1921.

Sweet Home Rosewood: Lost in the Fire. Retrieved January 14, 2003, from *The Seminole Tribune.* http://www.seminoletribe.com/tribune/99/may/rosewood.shtml.

TAKS: Texas Assessment of Knowledge and Skills. Retrieved September 15, 2003, from Texas Education Agency. http://www.tea.state.tx.us/student.assessment/taks/booklets/index.html.

Thomson, Tammie. *The Baobab Tree.* Retrieved April 9, 2003, from The Baobab Tree. http://www.inin.essortment.com/boabbaobabtree_rjlt.htm.

Traditional Proverbs. Retrieved March 10, 2003, from African Culture.dk. http://www.africanculture.dk/gambia/proverbsall.htm.

Trelease, Jim. *The Read-Aloud Handbook.* (4th Ed). New York: Penguin Books, 1995.

Tweed, Thomas A. *Islam in America: From African Slaves to Malcolm X.* Retrieved February 15, 2003, from Teacher Serve®. http://www.nhc.rtp.nc.us/serve/twenty/tkeyinfo/ islam.htm.

Twi Translations. Retrieved November 14, 2002, from Kente Cloth Festival—Ghanaian Language Translations. http://www.kente.net/twi.shtml.

Uganda—History. Retrieved January 23, 2003, from African Studies. http://www.sas.ipenn.edu/African_Studies/AS.html.

Underground Railroad. Retrieved March 21, 2002, from African.com. http://www.african.com/articles/tt_276.htm.

The Underground Railroad. Retrieved April 25, 2002, from *National Geographic. UndergroundRailroad@nationalgeographic.com.* http://www.nationalgeographic.com/ railroad/tl.html.

Van Hunks. *Bewitched Forests and Waters of the VhaVenda.* Retrieved February 24, 2003, from Van Hunks. http://www.vanhunks.com/lowveld1/venda.

Van Leeuwen, David. *Marcus Garvey and the Universal Negro Improvement Association.* Retrieved February 15, 2003, from Teacher Serve. http://www.nhc.rtp.nc.us:8080/tserve/twenty/tkeyinfo/garvey.htm.

Venda, the Land of Legends. Retrieved February 24, 2003, from Pafuri River Camp. http://www.pafuri.co.za/area.htm.

Welcome to Djembe-L FAQ Glossary. Retrieved March 24, 2003, from Drums.org. http://www.drums.org/djembefaq/glossary.htm.

Winegarten, Ruthe. *Texas Slave Families.* Retrieved February 19, 2003, from Texas History, Texas Culture Reading Room. http://www.humanities-interactive.org/texas/rural/tx_slave_families.htm.

Wit, Dorothy de. *The Talking Stone: An Anthology of Native American Tales and Legends.* New York: Greenwillow, 1979.

Worku, Michael. *Ethiopian Proverbs.* Retrieved March 10, 2003, from the Ethiopia Home Page. http://unicorn.ncat.edu/~michael/vses/eth4000/know/prov.html.

Your Name in Twi. Retrieved November 14, 2002, from the Fiankoma Project. http://www.fiankoma.org/schoolsite/yourname.htm.

INDEXES
▼▼▼▼▼

DJELIS: AUTHORS

TALKING DRUMS: BOOKS

CAPTIVITY'S SONGS: SPIRITUALS

About the Author

Wanda Cobb Finnen (M.Ed Curriculum and Instruction, Reading Specialization, Tarleton State University; BA Spanish and English, Secondary Education, University of Mary Hardin-Baylor) began her professional career with Los Angeles Community Colleges Overseas on the Atsugi Naval Base and Camp Zama Army Base in Japan. Ms. Finnen has also taught reading, language arts, and ESL in Japan, Pikes Peak Community College at Fort Hood, Texas, and for the Killeen and Belton Independent School Districts in Central Texas. She has served as a teacher trainer and mentor through the New Jersey Writing Project in Texas Writing Institutes. Born in Giessen, Germany, Wanda's appreciation for the diverse cultures of the world evolved as a natural by-product of her multiethnic family tree and her life as a military dependent.